GROWING TOGETHER

D0487315

GROWING TOGETHER

*a salvationist guide to
courtship, marriage and family life*

Edited by
Shaw and Helen Clifton

International Headquarters of The Salvation Army
101 Queen Victoria Street, London EC4P 4EP

Copyright © 1984 The General of The Salvation Army
First published 1984
ISBN 0 85412 445 4

Cover design by Jim Moss

Printed in Great Britain by
The Campfield Press, St Albans

CONTENTS

Part Four: We believe in marriage

Appendices

Foreword

'THE Salvation Army affirms the New Testament standard of marriage, that is, the voluntary and loving union for life of one man and one woman to the exclusion of all others, this union being established by an authorised ceremony.'

This is the opening paragraph of a *Statement on Marriage* recently published by The Salvation Army. The statement was formulated by a Commission on Marriage, established at International Headquarters in December 1980 by my predecessor, General Arnold Brown. The first chairman of the commission was Commissioner Norman Marshall who was succeeded in June 1982 by Commissioner Albert Scott.

Among the tasks that have been assigned to the commission is the production of a new Salvation Army book on courtship, marriage and family life. The book was to be edited in the form of a symposium, incorporating articles by salvationists from many parts of the world, Captain Shaw Clifton being appointed as editor of the symposium.

I express my warm and sincere thanks to the salvationists who have supplied their valuable contributions to the book, and to Captain and Mrs Clifton who have edited the publication in such an admirable way.

The book has been given a very appropriate title, *Growing Together*. This title, as is pointed out in the preface, 'reflects the fact that we learn from one another and strengthen one another in the Lord'.

I recommend this new book to readers on the five continents, just as the contributors represent all of these continents. Whilst I would especially recommend the book to Christians contemplating marriage, I also hope that it will be used, both for individual study and as a textbook for group discussions, by many other readers from older teenagers upwards.

I am also convinced that married couples, looking for enrichment of their marriage relationship and family life, will greatly profit by studying the book.

General
London 1984

Preface

WE would not want you to imagine this preface being composed in an impersonal office cut off from the pressures of family life. In fact, it is being typed at home by a busy mum who now and then casts a rueful glance at the basket of ironing which awaits her attention. Soon the children will come bounding in from the holiday club conveniently run by the local Salvation Army corps and the unnatural peace of the house will be shattered.

Reading the invited contributions to the book has been an absorbing and sometimes moving experience. Material has come from far and wide as salvationists try to work out God's ideal of love and marriage in today's world.

Why is this book written by many people instead of one?

The international Salvation Army has a wide variety of experience and expertise on which to draw. The result is a book which no one person could have written. When it comes to human relationships, everyone is growing and learning and no one has all the answers. We are grateful to all the contributors, who have shared their insights and experience, have written on the topics requested of them and have generously allowed their work to be welded into one volume.

On some topics different points of view may emerge and these will help you make up your mind on what is right for you and your family. Now and then, different writers emphasise the same point: this repetition only serves to reinforce important truths.

How should the book be used?

We hope that it will appeal to all age groups, from older teenagers upwards, helping them to understand themselves and each other a bit better. We would like to think it could be given by an Army corps to any young couple about to be married, together with a copy of the Scriptures which they can use for reading and praying together.

Again, why not make it a basis for teaching or discussion? Certain chapters or paragraphs might well be used for a series of study groups where older teenagers, young married people or parents meet to share ideas and try to work out their attitudes to marriage and family life.

Many will want to read the book right through, but others will prefer to dip into it and select the parts most relevant to them. A subject index is provided at the back. Appended to each real-life story in Part Four are discussion points and questions for study and sharing.

Naturally a single book cannot hope to deal with all that could be said. If this one encourages people to think in a positive and Christian way about marriage and also to share anxieties and aspirations with one another then it will have achieved something worthwhile for God.

Growing Together is a title which reflects the fact that we learn from one another and strengthen one another in the Lord. Look at Paul's words: 'Firmly beneath you is the foundation, God's messengers and prophets, the corner-stone being Christ Jesus himself. In him each separate piece of building, properly fitting into its neighbour, *grows together* into a temple consecrated to the Lord. You are all part of this building in which God himself lives by his Spirit' (Ephesians 2:20-22, *J. B. Phillips*).

All the chapters—and the lives of those who have written them—try to bear witness to the truths of the Bible and to God's revelation of himself in Jesus Christ. There is no aspect of our lives in which God is not interested and which his grace cannot cleanse and enrich.

Shaw and Helen Clifton
London 1984

Had I the heavens' embroidered cloths,
Enwrought with golden and silver light,
The blue and the dim and the dark cloths
Of night and light and the half-light,
I would spread the cloths under your feet:
But I, being poor, have only my dreams;
I have spread my dreams under your feet;
Tread softly because you tread on my dreams.

William Butler Yeats

Reverence for personality is essential to Christianity.

Catherine Baird

Part One
We Love Each Other

'WE each came from a family with a different faith. We became salvationists when we were in our young teens. It was then through our young people's group meetings that we really came to know each other.

'Both being involved in our corps activities, we often saw each other. We also spent time going out together to visit friends and sometimes we went to parks where we just sat down and talked. As Christians, we were always selective about the places we visited. We never went out to any questionable places. We just loved to be together.

'We both wanted to enter the school for officers' training, so prior to entering the school we became engaged. After we were commissioned as Salvation Army officers we had to serve in the field far from each other for nine months before we got married. The length of time and the far distance that separated us made us realise more that we really needed each other. There was constant letter-writing and our love grew deeper.'

José and Thelma Aguirre (The Philippines)

'THE Bible says, "In all thy ways acknowledge him, and he shall direct thy paths" (Proverbs 3:6). Marriage is an important matter in one's life. "In all thy ways" includes also the field of marriage. This is true in both of our lives. God saw the end from the beginning and was making all things work together for our good because we both love God and trust him.'

Karunakara and Vijaya Rao (India)

'FOLLOWING our earlier encounters, which neither of us recalls very clearly, we were so little ready to come to any understanding that we lost sight of each other for several years, both of us being taken up by our work and our respective circle of friends. It was not until 10 years after our first encounter that we realised that we

1

were meant for each other. So we were not very young when we married, both of us being 30 at the time.

'Having lost 10 years we certainly saw no reason to delay our marriage; Mireille left her job and we were married after a few months' engagement. We set out on married life together with the experience of those who have already a good slice of life behind them and we had no difficulty in getting along with each other. No doubt those years on our own had helped each of us to recognise the essentials of life and we had learnt to assess things at their real value. We can each affirm now, even if we were not consciously aware of it at the time, that the main reason for our union is our common faith. We know that it is God who has brought us together and that our married happiness would have been incomplete without the shared communion of our faith.

'We are very close, and being able to share and live our new life together has brought us even closer. How we would love to be able to convince young couples—and those less young—that real union between a man and a woman is truly realised only when they are spiritually united. We have really experienced this because our commitment to the Army was made when we already had several years of married life behind us and we have been able to see the deepening of our love for each other that has resulted.'

Jean and Mireille Poitevin (France)

Love—what is it?

Major Ed Dawkins (Australia)

WHAT is it that makes a girl want to stand on a street corner by the hour with a newspaper boy? Why does a young fellow stand in the cold after dark talking to a girl over her front fence whilst his mother wonders why he is taking so long to come home from the youth club? Why does this happen to a boy or girl who a few months earlier said, 'I'll never marry; I'm not interested in that'?

Just as the dawn comes slowly, almost imperceptibly, so our sexuality begins to have its impact on our thinking, feeling, responding—indeed, our total personality.

Day by day, very small changes occur until, almost suddenly, the young person finds himself struggling to relate effectively to the people around him.

Has any young person quickly and easily learned how to respond to another, particularly to one of the opposite sex, without feeling awkward or causing the other person to feel un-comfortable? For many, the reaching out to another has resulted in clumsy rather than comfortable contact.

The Bible, as God's word, leaves us in no doubt about the sexual aspects of our being. Right at the beginning we are told, '. . . God created man in his own image, in the image of God he created him; male and female he created them' (Genesis 1:27, *RSV*).

From then on, the Bible returns over and over again to the matter of male and female sexuality. Its impact on relationships is dealt with directly, explicitly, matter-of-factly and always seriously. The wonder of what happens to two persons who allow their sexuality to have its full expression in their life together is thoroughly em-phasised: 'Therefore a man leaves his father and his mother and cleaves to his wife, and they become one flesh' (Genesis 2:24, *RSV*). 'For this reason a man shall leave his father and mother and be joined to his wife, and the two shall become one' (Matthew 19:5, *RSV*).

Our sexuality provides the foundation for more than physical unity. It is the basis for emotional, psychological and spiritual oneness. It contributes to the complete bonding of two personalities. Within this bonding, the two may experience the greatest heights of communion that can ever occur between two people and discover a secure relationship within which children can be born and nurtured.

In considering, therefore, the matters of dating, choosing a partner, courtship, engagement and so on, we do so accepting that sexuality is a dominant force within the whole personality and a wonderful aspect of our total being. We may find the growing awareness of sexuality awkward and difficult to handle, but if we come to full acceptance of it as part of God's gift to us and if we adjust to accommodate its place in our life, then we may the more easily cope with it and see it integrated with all other parts of life. 'And God saw every thing that he had made, and, behold, it was very good . . .' (Genesis 1:31).

From acquaintance to commitment

David Mace, with his wife Vera, has contributed much to an understanding of sexuality and marital relationship. In *Youth Looks Towards Marriage* he gives a succinct report of the development of boy-girl relationships through the early stages.

In early childhood, boys and girls have no difficulty in accepting each other and playing together. As they grow older, they lose interest in being with the opposite sex and in fact consider each other with disdain. What is happening is that they are emphasising their differences. Then a change comes and the differences that once separated them cause them to be more interesting to each other. At the same time the differences become even more distinct. Just as the development of the differences is caused by the release of sex hormones, so is the development of interest.

However, although there is interest in the opposite sex, the developing sexuality of each becomes a new factor that has to be integrated into the relationship. This takes a lot of time. At first, they get together in groups. The groups give safety and opportunities for boys and girls to get together, be near each other and enjoy that nearness without having to cope with the one-to-one situation for longer than can be endured. Gradually though, young persons can manage the one-to-one experience for longer periods until, by various means, they find ways to spend more time with the one they find attractive.

Throughout all this, the whole being is maturing. First the sex organs become functional to their full extent whilst the body continues to grow for some years. The mind develops, knowledge and experience are acquired and awareness of emotions increases.

Whilst looking for a mate is important, there is also a need for the growing individual to learn about himself—his own values, ideals, general interests and so on—for ultimately the matching of two persons must occur on the basis of something substantially more than physical attraction.

The human mind and spirit have a great capacity to accommodate differences between personality but, within the nearness of the marriage relationship, each couple will have their own tolerance level to differences. If a marriage is to succeed, the proportion of attraction-of-sameness must be sufficient to bear the tension and stress of the attraction-of-difference. So often the differences that were so attractive before marriage become aggravations after marriage.

The dating, going together, or going steady, provide that necessary time for two persons to get to know each other and indeed for each to know himself or herself better. The arrangement allows two persons to agree to separate, with the least hurt to each other. Either or both may discover that the attraction is not sufficient to sustain a successful relationship through the many years of marriage, or that they are simply not ready to contemplate a life's commitment.

Paul's advice that we be 'not unequally yoked together' (2 Corinthians 6:14) has a wider application than just in the matter of beliefs or common goals and values. Yet intrinsic to the idea of a yoke is the presence of differences between the two bearers. The yoke of marriage does not exclude differences. It accepts reasonable differences and accepts them so that the whole is greater than the sum of its parts.

It is worth noting that at the very time we are making the momentous decision about who will be our life-partner, we are also trying to answer the questions, 'Whom or what shall I serve; to what cause will I commit my life?' 'What shall I do with my life; what things are most important to me?'

Answering these questions to our own satisfaction and identifying another person who is happy to make room for our answers is a major event. We should not wonder at the difficulty any one person may have in getting the answers right. In other words, a person may have a number of friends of the opposite sex before a commitment by way of engagement is made.

5

What is love?

Unfortunately, neither the mass media nor the story-tellers of our culture give us much help in understanding this most wonderful of all human emotions. Perhaps we too easily accommodate some of the commoner narrow ideas. For example, experiencing sexual union is referred to as 'making love'. The fact is that sexual union can range anywhere between nothing to do with love to its highest expression for a married couple. Certainly, the love that most seek as a basis for marriage is broader than physical attraction and desire for sexual expression. It speaks of wanting to share the whole of what the other is—the full range of life experiences—together with a kindness, a gentleness and a regard for the other's feelings and needs.

It has been said that we are in love when the satisfaction or security of the other person becomes as significant as our own.

From babyhood we learn about loving. At first we love according to our needs but later, if we have learned correctly, we are able to begin to love people not just for what they can give us. Thus true, mature love is not based simply on physical and emotional need. Indeed it should be held suspect if it lacks any part of 1 Corinthians 13:4-7 (*New English Bible*):

> Love is patient; love is kind and envies no one. Love is never boastful, nor conceited, nor rude; never selfish, not quick to take offence. Love keeps no score of wrongs; does not gloat over other men's sins, but delights in the truth. There is nothing love cannot face; there is no limit to its faith, its hope, and its endurance.

Therefore, love is something more than a mixture of physical attraction and emotion. It is when a couple come to the point of happily being able to share all of each other and their future that they can make the commitment of engagement.

Physical relationships without commitment?

However people struggle to accept their sexuality and come to terms with it, there is an early awareness that its full expression in sexual union, with all its pleasures, is highly desirable when it occurs with a partner who is loved. On the other hand, notwith-standing today's 'liberal' attitudes towards sex, most people will concede that sexual union belongs to the marriage relationship and has a 'wrongness' outside that setting. And so two young people find themselves in conflict trying to resolve the issue of the rightness of sex within certain limits. Resolving the issue is not easy, especially as it generally has to be done when the sexual drive is being experienced at its strongest.

Physical relationships without love?

It is a sad fact that many young people get involved in casual sexual relationships which they afterwards regret. This kind of experimentation can cause psychological and sexual problems later. In addition, sexually transmitted diseases flourish with promiscuous sexual behaviour and these are always serious.

Any person who is worried because they have been involved in casual sex should seek confidential and Christian advice. Christian counsellors or Salvation Army officers will not be shocked by what they hear. They know about human nature and about the power of evil to entice even those who are trying to be good. They will tell you how to obtain medical advice if needed and, equally important, they can tell you how to find the power of Jesus Christ to cleanse and give you a new start.

Physical relationships before marriage?

Not many years ago, the restraining influence on premarital sex was the possibility of pregnancy. This is now lessened by the ready availability of contraception, although sadly there are still many unwanted babies born to unmarried girls and an ever-increasing number of abortions performed simply for convenience. The Salvation Army sees these as lessening the respect due to human life.

Even if contraception were practised and totally reliable, would it be right to embark on a full sexual relationship before the commitment of marriage? One proposition made by this present age is that a couple should experience each other very fully before marriage and even live together to check on compatibility. Such 'testing' is shortsighted for it overlooks two important points:

1 Ultimately, a marriage does not stand on how skilful two persons become in sex but rather on how skilful they are in knowing each other, communicating with each other, being in touch with and responding to the deepest feelings, thoughts and needs of the other. We can have a topsy-turvy view of marriage, for sexual competence is *not* the base upon which all else stands. Rather, sexual competence will crumble if it does not have as its base competence in relationships at a psychological and spiritual level. In any case, most women need a sense of permanence, security and belonging to bring them to full sexual awakening. To induce and exploit these feelings without commitment would be cruel indeed.

2 If a marriage is to develop into a beautiful union throughout the long years of togetherness, then each partner must have a high regard for

the other as he or she is now *and* be ready to sustain that regard
through all the changes to each personality that will surely develop as
the years come and go.

2

Getting married

Major and Mrs Phil and Keitha Needham (USA)

The wedding: a ceremony of sealed love

WHAT is the next step for the salvationist couple who have fallen in love and become engaged? We strongly urge that they get in touch with their corps officer—or another officer whom they respect or whose pastoral skills they value—and *request* premarital guidance and counselling. In addition to his or her work with them, that officer may also utilise other resources that are available; for example, premarital training groups.

We cannot emphasise too strongly the importance of pastoral help. Because the institution of marriage is on shaky ground in the modern world, the salvationist couple who decide upon marriage owe it to themselves to take advantage of every opportunity to build a solid foundation. Being salvationists does not render them immune to marital failure.

What has happened to the institution of marriage today? To begin with, many people are getting married who are ill-prepared for such a step. Never have the emotional demands on the marriage relationship been greater, but people's abilities to meet those demands have not increased proportionately. Another destabilising factor is that many enter into the marriage contract with no enduring commitment and are ready to bail out as soon as the first or second crisis comes. A society of disposable commodities has also spawned the disposable marriage. Many don't even consider marriage to be a worthwhile venture and opt instead for experimental 'cohabitations'. The relationship continues only as long as it is convenient and hassle-free. In a recent survey of the views of university students, one third rated marriage as an obsolete custom!

In the past, even unhappy marriages were held together by the external pressures of law, religion, public opinion and economic

9

necessity. Today, these pressures have been all but eliminated for many people. Most of the marriages that now 'last' are those in which two people really have something good going between them, believe in marriage as a sacred covenant, and are willing to make a big investment in the development of their relationship.

In this chapter we would like to help the salvationist couple build a good marriage by describing biblical teaching and utilising it to understand and interpret the Salvation Army marriage ceremony. (The Salvation Army articles of marriage are set out in an appendix.) We will approach marriage in two ways: first, as an expression of love, and second, as a sacred covenant. Included in each section will be indented paragraphs. These will deal with the marriage ceremony itself and include suggestions for the wedding which are consistent with the understanding of marriage which is being developed.

Marriage: an expression of love

Ephesians 5:21-33 is probably the most significant biblical passage on marriage. Here Paul teaches that for the Christian the key to the marriage relationship is found in its parallel to the relationship of Christ to his Church. A Christian marriage isn't built simply by the husband and wife trying to be good Christians. It is built by their patterning their relationship after that of Christ and his Church.

What is there about the love between Christ and his Church that unveils the nature and purpose of marriage? How is this love between Christ and his Church expressed, and how does this expression shape the character of the love between Christian husband and wife? Let us answer these questions by considering the Ephesians reference and other scriptural passages.

Love expressed in reverence

'Be subject to one another out of reverence for Christ' (Ephesians 5:21, *RSV*).

Mutual respect is basic to all Christian relationships. Self-assertion without the deepest consideration of others is contrary to the Christian way of life. If in a fallen world the natural offspring of familiarity is contempt, then marriage, the relationship of greatest familiarity, should be where the Christian best demonstrates the power of Christ to engender the deepest mutual respect. Marital love is reverent love.

Speaking sensitively in relation to the then common assumptions, and the socio-economic structures of marriage and the role of women in his day, Paul taught that it was the particular calling of the wife to demonstrate this reverent love: 'Wives, be subject to your husbands, as to the Lord' (verse 22). This does not mean that the husband was not to be subject to his wife. He was to be equally so. He was not to forget verse 21. But it was the responsibility of the wife to be an example of this aspect of love to her husband. He was to learn his reverence from her.

Paul did not teach that the husband was to subject his wife to himself. She would willingly subject herself. It would be a choice made in freedom. The beauty of this subjection would be not only that it taught the husband the meaning of reverence in love, but that it also gave witness to the subjection of the Church to its Lord—also a choice made in freedom. In honouring her husband, she honoured her Lord and encouraged her husband to do the same.

We do not teach the total subjection of the wife to the husband. It is only to her Lord that the wife is called to be completely subject. It would be disastrous for her to submit to her husband under all conditions. Wives who do so may be trying to avoid responsibility for their actions. When it comes down to a choice between God's will and her husband's, the wife shows the most respect for her husband by going the way of her Lord.

The love which sustains and nurtures a marriage must be based upon mutual respect, and mutual respect is most enhanced where there is mutual subordination in Christ. There is no place in a Christian marriage for the exaltation of one partner and the oppression of the other. Christ is to be exalted, and the two partners subordinate to him first and to each other second. Within the salvationist spectrum, there are differing approaches to marital roles—ranging from the 'traditional' to the 'egalitarian'—and this is as it should be. Salvationist couples should work out their own agreement about respective roles in relation to their social, cultural, professional and economic situation. Whatever that agreement may look like, the common factor which enables them best to fulfil God's purpose for their marriage is reverence to Christ and, through him, to one another.

This expression of love in subjection to the Lord and in subjection to one another is a unifying theme of the entire marriage ceremony. Subjection to the Lord and his purposes is strongly emphasised in the articles of marriage which are read at the commencement of the ceremony. The couple declare: 1: that the marriage has not been sought only for the sake of their own personal interest; 2: that the marriage will not be allowed to lessen devotion to God and service for Christ; 3: that the partners will do their utmost to promote one another's self-

11

sacrifice for the cause of Christ; and 4: that the new home will become a place of divine worship and training for Christian service.

The mutual subordination of the couple in love is emphasised in the promise verbally made by both partners. Neither vows to relinquish more or less than the other. Neither will put his or her own interests before those of the other. Each pledges to love, comfort, honour, and keep. Subjected to their Lord, the couple find love's freedom—the freedom to subject themselves to one another.

Love expressed in sacrifice

'Husbands, love your wives, as Christ loved the church and gave himself up for her' (Ephesians 5:25, *RSV*).

For the Christian, sacrificial love may be called for in any human relationship, but it is an indispensable ingredient in the marriage relationship. Paul teaches that this form of love is the particular responsibility of the husband. In a society where husbands had almost absolute power over their wives, Christ called upon husbands to see their primary responsibility as making sacrifices for their marriage partners. This command is for modern husbands too. Here again, both partners are called upon to sacrifice for one another. But according to Paul, the husband is to lead the way. His role is not self-assertion but self-sacrifice, not dictatorship but devotion. He is constantly to be aware of Christ's love for his Church and to exemplify that love in the way he loves his wife. By doing so, he calls all Christians to active, sacrificial love.

If Christ's self-sacrifice is the means by which the Church is cleansed and made righteous, then in a similar way, says Paul, the sacrifices a husband makes for his wife add strength and purity to the marriage. In this day of the woman's greatly improved social status, the admonition to self-sacrifice in marriage must also apply to her. No longer can we just assume that she will sacrifice herself for him. She has other options available. Marriage counsellors have traced many marital breakdowns to an unwillingness of one or both partners to make significant sacrifices for the other and for the relationship. A marriage is purified and strengthened when the partners give up something they can have alone for something they can have together.

In the order of service for marriage, having made their promises to the presiding officer, the couple face each other and state before all witnesses present that they have willingly taken the other as their spouse and that in doing so out of love, they are accepting both the satisfactions and the sacrifices of the ongoing relationship '. . . for better for worse, for richer for poorer, in sickness and in health, to love and to cherish. . .'.

12

Love expressed in union

'For this reason a man shall leave his father and mother and be joined to his wife, and the two shall become one. This is a great mystery and I take it to mean Christ and the church . . .' (Ephesians 5:31, 32, *RSV*).

Man and woman were meant for each other. In the creation story, God looks down upon Adam in the garden, and concludes, 'It is not good that the man should be alone; I will make him a helper fit for him' Genesis 2:18, *RSV*). He puts Adam into a trance and from the same bone and flesh creates woman. Waking from his sleep and beholding this gift of a partner—like him, and yet so different—Adam exclaims in hushed wonder, 'Now this, at last!' (Genesis 2:23, paraphrase). Within that simple, spontaneous exclamation are contained all the attraction, wonder and mystery of the marriage relationship. At its deepest level, sexual attraction is the longing of two to become one. Only in the committed relationship of marriage can that desire be fulfilled.

'Union' and 'unity' are very important words for the Christian. They point to the goal of human history in Christ (Ephesians 1:9, 10). The consequence of sin is separation of men from God and from one another. Christ's mission is to unite us again: 'For he is our peace, who hath made both one, and hath broken down the middle wall of partition . . .' (Ephesians 2:14). Those who are united in him are his fellowship, his Church, and their mission is to bring the message of reconciliation in Christ to a separated world. The Church can fulfil this mission because it is his creation and not its own.

So it is with marriage. A Christian marriage is not the creation of two people; it is the creation of Jesus Christ. It is a marriage patterned not primarily after the type of marriage their parents had—however good that marriage may have been—nor the types of marriages prevalent in society at that particular time. It is primarily patterned after Christ's marriage to his Church.

Helen Papanek, a marriage therapist, said that the one basic conflict that characterises all marriage neuroses is 'the need for closeness and the fear of it'. If it is a sign of our sinfulness that there is separation between us, it is a sign of our salvation that we are coming closer together. Nowhere are the signs of the sinfulness, and the salvation, more visible than in the marriage relationship. It seems to us, therefore, that nowhere more than in the Christian's marriage does God want to reflect the reality of reconciliation through Christ.

Marital unity in Christ is powerfully symbolised in the ceremony when the bride and bridegroom place the rings on one another's hands. The rings themselves, of course, are symbolic of unbroken unity and the act of exchanging rings is a testimony to the couple's commitment to unity in love. But notice also that the trinitarian name of God is invoked: '. . . in the name of the Father, and of the Son, and of the Holy Spirit'. God himself is a unity of three. Being three, he is also one. It is within the reality of this God who is Three in One that the fellowship of believers, though many, can be one, and two people, though sexually opposite, can become one in marriage. This is the union which real love craves.

Love expressed in diversity

'So God created man in his own image . . . male and female . . .' (Genesis 1:27).

In their sexuality men and women reflect the image of God. Just as God the Father chooses to realise himself only in relation to himself, the Son, and the Holy Spirit (the persons of the Trinity), and to those beings whom he creates, even so man realises God's intention for his life only in relation to God and to other human beings. Man finds himself only when he finds someone else. We were created for relationships. The relationships in which we tend to grow the most are those with persons who are different from us, and the most basic natural difference between us is sexual. That is why the marriage relationship offers one of the greatest opportunities for personal development. Good marriage partners enable each other to see and understand themselves more fully and to grow into something better.

Love expressed in diversity means that each partner in the marriage allows the other to be different—in sexuality, personality, interest and sociability. It also means that cultural stereotypes of sexuality are not foisted on the other. Diversity in marriage is for the partners to respond openly to one another, to become richer by sharing that which makes them so different, to become a mirror through which each can better find himself, and by doing so, to bring each other closer to God. The paradox of marriage is that marital union is best realised where each partner's differences are most appreciated and affirmed.

This mutual appreciation of differences will enrich decision-making within the marriage. The ceremony itself should be planned with that appreciation in mind. There is an essential order of service for marriage in The Salvation Army and the presiding officer is responsible for seeing to it that spiritual dimension and scriptural teaching are not compromised. However, within these requirements

14

the couple have ample opportunity to have their say about the service. The engaged couple will want to discuss the service at length, each with deep sensitivity to the desires of the other. Here are some of the important matters about which they must make decisions:

1 Who will perform the ceremony? When and where will it take place? Ideally, the person chosen to perform the ceremony will not only be a significant pastor in the life of one or both partners, he or she will also be someone who is likely to be available for counsel in the early months of the marriage. The location is likely to be a place of significance in the life of one or both partners, and salvationists will almost invariably wish to be married in their local Salvation Army hall.

2 What Scriptures will be read? In searching the Scriptures for marital guidelines, the couple will find passages that are particularly helpful. One or two may even be adopted as thematic for their marriage. The choice of Scripture for the wedding will then come naturally.

3 What congregational songs will be sung and what other types of music used? (There is a special section for weddings in *The Song Book of The Salvation Army*.) Special music can be provided by voice and/or instrument. We suggest careful discrimination in the matter of sentimental secular songs which tend to make their appearance at too many weddings.

4 Who will be in the wedding party and who will take care of other arrangements and responsibilities? Usually, friends and relatives are chosen for these roles.

It is important that the couple discuss these matters not only with each other but also with the officer who will be officiating. The officer is finally responsible for the service. But if the couple have been involved in the planning, the service will be an expression of the individuality of each enhanced by the unity of both.

Love expressed in nurturing

'Be fruitful, and multiply . . .' (Genesis 1:28).

It is God's intention that marriages become a source of nourishment to others. We are speaking first of all of children who are born to, or adopted by, the couple. The growing love of a married couple becomes a cup running over which nourishes the children. However, we speak also of all who come in contact with the couple—those who find strength, encouragement, guidance or healing in the love overflowing from the marriage.

One of the marks of a healthy marriage is that others are enriched by it. The idea of a private marriage is contrary to the gospel. Although marriage has to do with a lifelong relationship between one man and one woman, its purpose in God's plan is far wider. Do not many romantic stories of couples falling in love end with the wedding? All that is said about their subsequent history is that 'they lived happily ever after'. This popular myth tends to limit the marriage to the couple concerned. In truth, the wedding is but a beginning and, if the marriage grows as God intends, it will bring a far-reaching influence and involvement in the lives of others. Where there is a lifelong relationship of love expressed in reverence, self-sacrifice, oneness and mutual appreciation, there is a witness to the world of God's gracious action in the lives of two people, there is an example for others to follow, and there is strength from which others can draw.

We suggest, therefore, that the wedding be a community affair, a testimony to the fact that both partners recognise that their marriage implies a larger responsibility in marriage to those who are present and all whom they will have the opportunity to influence. It is not out of place, therefore, for the officer to include in his concluding volley: 'God bless your relatives and friends!'

Marriage: a sacred covenant

A covenant is an agreement between two parties in which they pledge themselves in loyalty to one another. It is more than an agreement to carry out certain external actions (as in a contract); it is also a pledge of faithfulness and commitment. Marriage is a sacred covenant between two people in love. The wedding is a celebration of this covenant, a public recognition that this love has been sealed for life. The focus of the ceremony is in the covenant vows made by the couple, vows which define both the privileges and the responsibilities of the covenantal partners.

At the very beginning of the service, the presiding officer calls attention to the articles of marriage (see appendix) the seriousness of which is heralded at the commencement: 'We do solemnly declare . . .'. After repeating the articles, he then turns to the couple and says, 'If you wish to be married upon these terms, please stand forward.' The covenant requires a voluntary act of the will. His next words to the couple are an exhortation to enter into this relationship only with integrity and seriousness of heart. In response the couple give assurance that there is no impediment of law or conscience to entering into this marriage covenant. Then, when the promises and declarations have been made, the covenant is symbolically sealed with the rings and the joining of hands.

A covenant with God

'We are gathered here in the sight of God. . . .'

If early salvationist weddings placed so much emphasis upon the marriage serving the purposes of the salvation war that it seemed that the development of the marriage relationship itself was not important, we should not allow the pendulum to swing so far in the other direction that it seems that what matters is only the partners' commitment to each other.

Marriage is first of all a covenant with God. The Bible clearly teaches that it was instituted by God for man and that it was to be one of the important means by which mankind was to fulfil God's purpose. As instituted by God, it requires God's direct participation and guidance. As instituted for the benefit of man, it requires that the couple live together in obedience to God. In no way should God be left out of any aspect of this covenant. Marriage is not an end in itself. Ultimately, its purpose is to bring two people closer to God and to his purposes for their lives.

The marriage ceremony is first and foremost a service of worship. The word of God is read and prayer is offered. Before the vows are made, the presiding officer reminds everyone present that they 'are gathered here in the sight of God'. The charge to the couple is made 'in the presence of God, who searches all hearts'. The couple promise 'to live together after God's ordinance'. The declarations to one another are made 'according to God's holy ordinance' and upon their honour as 'true soldier(s) of Jesus Christ'. In the ring ceremony, the vows are sealed in the threefold name of God. The two are joined 'in the name of God'. Then comes what is perhaps the weightiest statement in the service: 'Whom God hath joined together, let no man put asunder!' It is God, in all his grace and power, who seals this covenant and makes it possible for two people to keep it. The closing prayer, appropriately, is a plea to him for help, and the final blessing is his.

God is recognised in every aspect of the service. This is true not only of the words that are said but also of the symbols which are seen. The Salvation Army flag is prominent, symbol of our faith in God. The ceremony takes place near the mercy seat, symbol of our reliance upon God's mercy and reminder to all of their covenant with God. In addition, we recommend that salvationist couples wear either uniform, which is a symbol of their Christian commitment, or tasteful dress which leans toward simplicity and avoids garish display.

In the early days, both the bride and the groom were expected to give their testimonies, and the service concluded with an invitation to the mercy seat. If we today reject this utilitarian use of the wedding for evangelistic purposes as an inappropriate distraction from the marriage covenant itself—a covenant whose durability is not taken for granted as it once was—we should not lose the underlying point: the most important covenant for all of us is our covenant with God, and it is God who is the author of, and who authenticates, any marriage covenant. As the mercy seat is the focal point of all other Army meetings, so it is of the marriage ceremony. From first to last, marriage is God's miracle.

17

A covenant with one another

'I do take thee. . . .'

As a covenant, marriage requires an equal commitment from both partners, an equal acceptance of responsibility for the well-being and growth of the relationship, and an equal division of role responsibilities. Whether the couple assume roles in accord with a more traditional pattern where responsibilities are predetermined, or in accord with the more egalitarian pattern where roles are negotiated and can be renegotiated, the covenant requires accountability from both partners. In marriage each takes the other of his or her own free will. Two people move toward each other for life, and this movement is a sign that the brokenness of sin, the mark of fallen man, is on the way to being mended. Marriage between Christians is a covenant freely entered into, firmly founded upon mutual trust. As such, it reflects the character of God's new saving covenant in Christ.

> In the marriage service, the officer pointedly directs a series of questions to each partner respectively: 'Will you have . . .?' The service can proceed no further unless each responds, 'I will!' There must be assurance that the couple understand and accept this union as a relationship they have freely chosen for life. It is their covenant with one another before God.

> (In recent years some couples have eliminated the custom of the father or parents of the bride 'giving her away'. The reason is usually to emphasise that the choice of a marriage partner has been made freely by mature individuals.)

> Then they turn to face each other. The vows become personal. They declare their love, a love that will not be diminished by either prosperity or adversity, a love that endures.

A covenant before the community

'I call upon these persons here present. . . .'

Marriage between Christians is a covenant relationship with a social dimension. First, the entire family of each partner is involved. The expression 'marrying into the family' suggests that the marriage alters and broadens the structure of each family. Inter-family relationships are redefined. Family members should be involved in the wedding. Because the marriage affects their lives, participation in the celebration also helps them to adjust to the change.

Second, the friends of both partners, and comrade salvationists, are also involved. This union will affect their lives, and they will have some influence on it in the years to come. Their presence and support are vital.

Third, the entire community is involved. Few within it may know the couple, but any of them may come under the influence of this marriage. As we suggested earlier, the couple have a larger responsibility. Their marriage is to be a source of nurture to others, a reflection of the divine covenant, and a means of witness. It is God's desire that the Christian's covenant of marriage be a means of leading people into a covenant relationship with him.

This is why the marriage vows are said before the people. 'These persons here present' are called upon not only to witness the exchange of vows but also to pledge their support to this union, to affirm their belief in this divinely ordained institution and to serve as a reminder to the couple that their marriage involves a social responsibility and a mission to the larger community. Hence, before the vows are said, the officer says to those who are present, '*We* are gathered here in the sight of God to join this man and this woman. . .'. Even the secular law does not recognise as valid a marriage ceremony performed without witnesses.

Without disparaging the wishes of some to have private weddings with only a handful in attendance, we do want to urge the value of a more 'public ceremony', allowing salvationists and other friends the opportunity to be supportive, providing a visible witness of marriage as a Christian covenant and making it possible for others to be blessed and strengthened by the service. There are a lot more things going on in the hearts of those who are present at a Christian wedding than any one person would ever be able to perceive. Something is being confirmed in the lives of some who have been on their marriage pilgrimage for years. Perhaps a couple who are having difficulty are being helped. Young singles who may yet face the decision of whether or not to marry are being taught by what they are witnessing. And most importantly, the couple making their promises are being strengthened by this wider support.

The wedding is a community affair. The reception which many couples choose to have following the service is an opportunity both to celebrate the happy occasion and to reinforce the social dimension of what has taken place. We think that avoidance of the lavish can help to facilitate this communal aspect of the reception. Undistracted by excessive displays and refreshments and put at ease by an atmosphere of informality, friends can freely express their alcohol-free affection, offer words of encouragement and pledge their support.

A covenant for life

'. . . so long as you both shall live.'

At the very beginning of this chapter, we noted that the institution of marriage had fallen upon hard times. Trial marriages are common, and divorces are easy to obtain. But marital failure also comes to many who married with every intention of staying together for life. The couple, it seems, were not prepared for what they were getting into, or found that they were unable or unwilling to make the personal investment that a successful marriage relationship requires nowadays.

We take the position that when two people marry, God intends the relationship to be for life. Divorce is never God's will. It is impossible to find the slightest shred of scriptural justification for the view that God's word to the newlyweds is, 'Give it a good try, and if you don't make it, seek a divorce.' Marriage is a divine institution; divorce is a human addendum. Jesus taught that man should not put asunder what God had joined together. But then he added that because of the Israelites' hardness of heart, Moses had allowed men to divorce their wives (Matthew 19:3-9). Divorce is a human reality of which God does not approve, but which he permits as a concession to human weakness. When a marriage has failed and there seems to be no hope of salvaging it after serious efforts have been made, he accepts the reality of what has happened, and he makes himself available to the separating partners as they confess their shortcomings and set out to build a new life. He does not abandon his own when they are most in need of healing and reaffirmation.

What we wish to emphasise is that unless the newly-weds approach their marriage as a lifelong commitment, it is unlikely that their relationship will survive even the assaults that will come, let alone be strengthened by them. Instead, the couple will tend to 'bail out' and thereby avoid the risk of intimacy and change and self-sacrifice which marital growth requires.

> Practically everything in the marriage ceremony points to this permanent aspect of the covenant. We caution against any tampering with the religious ceremony—or indeed with the secular—that would dilute the emphasis on durable commitment. Changing 'so long as we both shall live' to 'so long as we both shall love', for example, is a sentimental touch with a superficial basis. Many of our 'loves' change with the seasons of our lives, or are superseded by more powerful attachments. But there are loves that are meant to endure through life, and, like the relationship between Christ and his Church, the marriage relationship is one of them. Any lesser commitment is an arrangement to try something, but it is not marriage. Marriage is a covenant to risk something for life.

An exclusive covenant

'. . . from this day forward. . . .'
In relation to their sexuality, some are called to marriage and

others are called to the single life. Like all other callings, marriage entails a clear commitment to a purpose in God's plan. Specifically, it is a life commitment to live together in exclusive marital fidelity with a chosen partner of the opposite sex.

What do we mean by marital fidelity? First, we mean spiritual fidelity: the couple pledge their commitment to God and the pursuit of his will for their lives and for their marriage. Second, we mean social fidelity: the couple pledge to maintain a home together, share their resources and spend most of their social time together. And third, we mean sexual fidelity: the couple pledge that although friendships with the opposite sex are allowed, sexual activity (and this does not mean only sexual intercourse) is confined to the marriage partner.

These and other aspects of marital commitment should be thoroughly discussed and agreed upon by both partners before the wedding takes place. Each partner brings different expectations to the marriage. Where assumptions conflict, negotiation should take place and agreement be reached in the light of scriptural guidelines and advisedly with pastoral help. Marriage is an important calling for which careful preparation should be made.

We hope that what has been said in this chapter will encourage salvationist readers contemplating marriage to approach this relationship as a divine calling, to understand it from a biblical perspective, to explore the meaning of their wedding as a true reflection of their faith and commitment, to take an honest look at their relationship and to open the lines of communication.

3

Let's talk about choosing a Christian partner

Colonel and Mrs David and Alice Baxendale (USA)

DAVID: I once asked a group of businessmen, 'If you gave as much time trying to improve your business as you do trying to improve your marriage, what kind of shape would your business be in?' Several of the men's faces turned red. They realised they gave a great deal of attention to developing their career, but little creative thought to developing their marriage relationship.

Alice: A. W. Tozer said, 'The bent of nature is toward the wild, not toward the fruitful field.' If you let a garden go, the weeds will take over. The same thing will happen in a marriage. If you do just what comes naturally and no more, your relationship deteriorates. You find yourselves getting further and further apart. Dave and I have been married for 30 years, but what we have to share with you is not a boatload of great successes and testimonies about what we've done right. Some of the greatest lessons we have learned have come through tears and heartache.

David: We believe God intended marriage to be the closest human relationship on earth. We really believe God intends a man's best friend to be his wife, and a woman's best friend to be her husband—though they can have other good friends as well.

Alice: A marriage between Christians is a total commitment of two people to the person of Jesus Christ and to one another. Every part of this definition is significant. Marriage is a commitment in which there is no holding back anything. We live in a day when commitments are taken lightly, when somehow it seems all right to figure out a way to justify not following through with them.

Marriage is a commitment to Jesus Christ. When two objects are close to a third object, they are of necessity close to each other. When you and your wife or husband become close to Christ, you are of necessity closer to one another.

22

David: A Christian marriage should free the man and woman to be themselves, and to become all that God intends them to become.

I believe my own personality and my sense of inner well-being have been greatly enhanced over the 30 years that Alice has invested herself in my life. In contrast, if a marriage relationship is causing one member to freeze up and to hide his or her true self, to feel unfulfilled, then it might be because Jesus Christ is not being allowed to permeate that marriage.

Alice: The premise for this refining process that God has built into marriage is found in Genesis 2:18, when God said, 'It is not good that the man should be alone; I will make him an help meet for him.' God designated the wife to correspond to her husband, to blend with him so that they fit together.

After Dave and I had been married only a few months we could look back and see how God had led us together, but we wondered what in the world he had in mind. As we look back, it has been the most exciting spiritual journey, one we could never have imagined and as Catherine Marshall has stated, 'We have met God at every turn!'

David: Now, what about this business of marrying a non-Christian? Would you allow us to share with you some very blunt, frank and straightforward talk as an experienced married couple who have come to love and revere the word of God? For some, it may be hard medicine but this is how we see it.

The Salvation Army and the Christian marriage ceremonies are designed for Christian people. They do not make sense for unbelievers.

Alice: We have asked couples, 'Why do you want to be married in the Army, or the church, in the first place?' Sometimes they admit, with a sense of relief, 'Well, it's because my family wants me to; it is the expected thing.' We remind them that this is a moment for great integrity. It is not a time for sentiment alone. The marriage vows are solemn words—and they are taken before the eyes of the holy God whose gaze penetrates into our very hearts.

David: Christians desire to see the union of a man and woman expressed within the widest possible context, the context of the body of Christ and before the eyes of the creator, the redeeming God. They are the ones for whom the Christian marriage ceremony is designed.

Alice: When we look at marriage within that context, we learn that people are to be married, as the Army's ceremony book states, 'in the presence of God'. Scripture makes it clear that Christians are to marry only Christians. We say this clearly and without

23

equivocation: no Christian young man or young woman is led by the Spirit of God to marry an unbeliever.

David: Paul makes a flat command before he asks a series of questions: 'Do not be mismated with unbelievers.' Or, as it says in the *King James Version,* 'Be ye not unequally yoked together with unbelievers.' Then come the questions: 'For what fellowship hath righteousness with unrighteousness? and what communion hath light with darkness? And what concord hath Christ with Belial? or what part hath he that believeth with an infidel? And what agreement hath the temple of God with idols? for ye are the temple of the living God' (2 Corinthians 6:14-16).

Alice: So it is not the will of God for a Christian young person to marry a non-Christian. People easily delude themselves into thinking, 'Well, you don't know how nice she is. She is a very sweet girl. She's wonderful, and she's better than some Christians I know.' Or you might argue, 'Surely after a little while she'll be won to faith in Jesus Christ. I am sure that God is leading us in this direction.'

David: We have to suggest to you, 'No, God is not leading you in that direction. It will probably not work out. You will enter marriage with anticipation, joy and expectancy, but it may collapse on the rocks.' You will wonder why. The Holy Spirit will hardly ever lead you, if you are a Christian, to marry someone who is not a Christian, even with the fond hope that such a person will later be won to the Lord. Sometimes that actually happens, but too often it is the Christian partner who is adversely influenced. You see, if you do not obey the Spirit you step out from under the will of God. You are on your own. Step out of the purpose of God and you have no guarantee that God will make all things work for good. (See also the story told in Chapter 14.—*Eds.*)

Alice: The Scripture informs us that there is a total and absolute distinction before God between a believer and one who is not a believer. One has passed from death unto life. The other remains in the grip of sin. They belong to two different kingdoms.

David: You can't tell by looking at a person whether or not he or she is a Christian. We are prepared to admit that some non-Christians have such a generous portion of the common grace of God that they act in a more Christian way than some Christians we know. However, there is an absolute separation between the two in the sight of God.

Alice: The distinction is not in terms of those whose names are or are not inscribed on Army membership rolls. The question is, 'Do you have faith in Jesus Christ, and have you received him into your life?' This is the message that has to be accepted. Someone can hold

24

out to you a gift with your name on it, but if you do not receive it, it is not yours. It's the same with the gift of God's grace. He does not thrust it upon you. Nobody can make you a Christian. Your parents can't do it. Your officer or pastor can't do it. Only the Holy Spirit does it, in response to your faith in Jesus Christ. We are aware that there are people who have come to the Lord after they were married, and as a result there is one Christian partner and a non-Christian. The Scripture speaks about that. It says that if the unbeliever wishes to remain with the believer, then that is what should happen (1 Corinthians 7:13). The Bible also declares the possibility (1 Peter 3:1, 2) of the unbelieving partner being won over by the quiet witness of the believer. Sometimes one partner of a Christian marriage may backslide in their faith, to the point of becoming an unbeliever. Then the one who is still a Christian needs all the wisdom and grace of God to maintain a definite but unprovocative witness.

David: If you are a Christian, you will be concerned to find the right person to marry. Do you believe that God has someone for you? Do you dare to trust your life into his hands in finding a mate? Do you dare to say, 'Lord, I believe that you have someone for me. I don't know who it is, but I want the person of *your* choice?'

Part Two
We are husband and wife

'IT has been said that if we base our marriage on romantic love alone, we would re-word the marriage vows. Instead of saying "as long as we both shall live" we might well say "until we get bored with each other". The only firm foundation is the Lord Jesus Christ.

'As we are called to love our neighbours, my wife is my nearest neighbour. I know her hopes, her fears, her aspirations, when she is strong and when she is weak, just as Christ knows me. Sometimes when I have been in distress my wife has drawn my attention to the cross, shown me a picture of Christ and asked me, "What is Jesus telling you?" Thus we encourage each other.'

Joseph Larbi (Ghana)

'ONE has not "arrived" just because he becomes a husband, or she a wife. There must be a striving to become that type of husband or wife that is God's ideal. Husbands and wives have to keep in mind that they become a type of VIP (very important person) when they are married—a VIP to their partner. However, although this must be the ideal, it is not automatically so if they do not work at it, striving ever to continue to be, and to grow as, that special person for the partner. A true Christian, in the act of believing, does become a VIP. And this sets the true basis for their role in the marriage partnership.'

Antonio and Giovanna Longo (Italy)

4

The sexual relationship

Lieut-Colonel (Dr) Sidney Gauntlett (Great Britain)

WE bring into any relationship our own temperament and all that the years that have gone before have contributed to our personality. This is especially so within marriage and more particularly in its most intimate aspect, the sexual relationship. Each partner contributes a different disposition, style of upbringing, set of values and total personality. These differences can enrich and strengthen the relationship as they complement each other or they can create difficulties, placing the relationship under a strain.

This happened with John and Mary, a young Christian couple who were very much in love and had looked forward eagerly to their wedding. They had been happy to show their affection for each other in kissing and cuddling and Mary had been a virgin when she married. Both John and Mary believed that it was right and in keeping with their beliefs to keep a deeper sexual relationship until after their marriage. Apart from the fact that Mary became embarrassed when he tried to talk about the physical side of their marriage or discuss family planning, John had no idea of any problem Mary might have with the sexual side of their relationship. Both were keen to have children.

A year later they both sought help and it seemed as though much of the radiance had gone from their marriage. They had not yet been able to consummate it and tensions were mounting between them. In John's home his parents were a warm couple who often showed their love for each other when others were around and so the children felt warm and secure within the family. Sex was easily talked about without embarrassment. Mary's family was more reserved. She was the only child and her father was strict and very protective towards his daughter whilst her mother was shy. Her parents, although happy together, never showed their affection for each other in Mary's presence. She grew up to feel that sex was something almost shameful, surrounded by a mystique that suggested fear. The honeymoon to which they had looked forward was distressing for both. John, who recognised Mary's shyness, approached intercourse carefully and gently but even the exposure of her body to John, whom she loved dearly, was upsetting and every attempt at intercourse failed because of Mary's tenseness. She was able to enjoy some of the love play before and hated herself for what she was doing to John. She just could not explain why she reacted as she did and tried hard to assure John that it was not directed against him because she really loved him. At first, he was able to accept this, but in time accusation was met with counter-accusation and the tension grew. Only after a year of unhappy struggle did they agree together to seek help.

Such difficulties can be overcome if the couple can be helped to look honestly and sensibly at themselves and their backgrounds. John and Mary are part of a minority and for most couples there are no great difficulties which they cannot sort out themselves. Marriage and sex should never be seen as problems but as an exciting adventure. Nevertheless, problems do arise and there are many misunderstandings associated with sex.

Sex—God's gift to his children

Sex is probably one of the most misused words in most languages. Its use often implies that it represents an isolated part of human feeling and behaviour—a sport or a perversion, to be enjoyed or endured. Many talk of 'making love' when they don't really mean love but something purely physical and often selfish, more akin to lust. Our attitudes are governed very largely by our upbringing and the ideas and standards of those close to us. Some people regard sex as the most important aspect of marriage and believe that the full expression of our sexuality is the key to true happiness. Others, like Mary, view it with a sense of fear and even guilt and certainly not something to be spoken of easily. For many Christians it can present a perpetual struggle and some still think of their sexuality as nature's strongest competitor against a spiritual faith, acting as if there couldn't possibly be any connection between God and sex. But God gave us our sexuality as one of his most precious gifts, as a trust to be used as he intended; it is a unique gift from him for our personal pleasure and joy and the continuity of his family on earth.

Our sexuality is an integral part of our whole personality. Genetic studies show that every part of our body carries evidence of our sexuality which also enters into each dimension of life—our physical, emotional and spiritual being. Jesus, speaking of marriage, said 'and the two shall be one flesh' and Paul uses this intimate union of male and female—the bride and bridegroom—to illustrate the union of a loving Christ with his Church.

In giving us this gift, God wants us to find deep joy, freedom from fear, a rich relationship and the development of family life through new lives born. In this way there is a perpetuation from generation to generation of the gifts and graces he has bestowed upon us. For very many the sexual attraction is a natural part of a relationship between a man and woman preparing to marry, whether the relationship is based upon 'spontaneous' love or on a family arrangement as applies in some cultures. For some, sex is seen as the main part of a marriage and sexual attractiveness as the most important consideration in choosing a marriage partner. If this attractiveness is seen in purely physical terms (beautiful looks, perfect figure, good physique—'tall, dark and handsome') then such couples are likely to meet troubles. Life together as man and wife is a great deal more than sex, and the disillusionment that comes when the fantasy of idyllic romance fades as hair turns grey (or disappears!), wrinkles appear and the body becomes fat and flabby, may rob the relationship of all its romance and warmth. But sexual attractiveness goes much deeper than this and is seen in the whole personality, not just the physical features.

A marriage relationship involves all three dimensions of body, mind and spirit, each interacting on the others. Neglect in one dimension affects the others and a truly loving relationship between a man and a woman involves their total lives so that each enriches the other in all dimensions. When Jesus spoke of two being one flesh he was not implying that physical or sexual union was the most important, but all we read in the Bible of such relationships tells us that in a loving relationship the union of mind and spirit is expressed in sexual union, and that this should be pleasurable. This gives divine approval to a physical sexual union and it also means that when we are out of harmony emotionally or spiritually sexual harmony is likely to be impaired. Similarly, if there is sexual frustration or disunity there is likely to be an adverse reaction in the mental and spiritual relationship.

Sexual expectations

What is in the minds of most couples as they approach their wedding? The excitement at the prospect of total sharing and abandonment to each other. The prospect of a perfect honeymoon when for the first time they will enjoy each other's bodies without restraint to full sexual intercourse with its exhilarating satisfaction and fulfilment. The thought of living happily ever after in constant marital and sexual bliss! Doubtless no reader was quite as starry-eyed as this. Some may even have grown cynical, anxious or fearful, like Mary and John. Others, who at first achieved happiness and harmony in their sexual relationship, may have allowed this to become stale or even boring. Even in these days, with sex education and information readily available, there are those whose marriage is being spoilt by ignorance or the recall of past hurtful experiences. Embarrassment, guilt or even fear deny that lovely sexual closeness which should lie at the heart of every marriage and these emotions may be compounded by clumsiness and insensitivity by the other partner. Even a basic loving relationship may not prevent hurt and even havoc if these feelings are allowed to continue.

Much suffering and misunderstanding could be prevented by careful pre-marriage counselling arranged by the Salvation Army officer or minister who conducts the wedding followed by sensitive pastoral care of the young married couple. Unhappily, feelings of failure or shame are common amongst Christians but skilled counselling, if sought in time, can usually help in the restoration and development of a truly happy and liberated relationship. Even if preparation for marriage may not deal with specific sexual techniques it should encourage a free expression of uncertainties, fears and even past hurts in a relaxed and understanding atmosphere.

A fear of unwanted pregnancy may prevent a satisfying relaxed sexual relationship and the answer lies simply in informed family planning (see chapter 6) before marriage. It is surprising how often, even in these days, this is neglected.

There are those couples who see marriage simply as a partnership or companionship which, although loving and even warm, does not include any real sexual relationship. Although very uncommon, if this is the sincere wish of both partners they can be very happy, even though most people would feel that such a relationship must be deprived of that deeper richness that God intends. More often than not it is only the one partner that would settle for a non-sexual relationship and the other has to try to cover up frustration and disappointment, usually leading to tension.

Amongst couples who engage in intercourse before marriage, either on isolated occasions when their feelings run away with them or regularly, one or both partners may start their marriage with feelings of guilt or furtiveness associated with their sexual relations so that intercourse may not be as relaxed or spontaneous as it could be. When sexual feelings dominate during courtship other aspects of the relationship are neglected, so they may hardly know each other except sexually. When they begin to face life together in all its aspects and responsibilities they see a very different partner and may not like what they see—little more than a pretty face or a tough and handsome body!

God's will—our pleasure

This marvellous gift called sex is a recognition that it is God's will that we should procreate and build families and homes where children can be nurtured in love and security. But we recognise that sexuality is not only for the production of children but also for our pleasure and joy. The puritanical concept that sexual relationships were a concession to our human frailty and certainly not to be enjoyed is a travesty. The Bible does not teach this. We might ask why there is naturally such exquisite physical and emotional pleasure in sexual intercourse in a loving relationship if it is meant to be merely endured. Fullness of joy and satisfaction in relaxed and spontaneous sexual relations is what God intends, if shared by two people who truly love each other and who are fully committed to each other within the security of marriage.

There are many potential pitfalls and hurts when such a depth of relationship is attempted outside marriage. We need to remember always that the act of sexual union is associated with potential creation of life and should therefore be counted as sacred.

The idea of testing each other out to ensure sexual compatibility is based on a myth that there is such a thing as fixed incompatibility, and in any case it is rarely a true test. Often the very factors that bring a couple—unintentionally for at least one partner—to intercourse during courtship are likely to cause problems in later marriage relations—selfishness, lack of sensitivity, self-indulgence. It is for all these reasons that the Bible speaks clearly against fornication. I have heard many young couples say how glad they were that they waited until after their wedding before sharing in this special sexual relationship.

Is there such a thing as sexual technique?

With all that we have said about love and spontaneity the concept of sexual technique seems out of place. But although we can achieve any relationship by the process of trial and error there is value in giving thought to certain guidelines and techniques. There can be hurt or impoverishment of the relationship through neglect and ignorance. From a purely physical point of view, sexual intercourse is simply the penetration of the woman's vagina by the male organ or penis. For the newly-wed couple, this full penetration alone can bring great excitement and a deep sense of emotional and even spiritual union. As with childbirth, there is a small price to be paid during the first attempt at intercourse as the membrane across the entrance to the vagina of a virgin has to be broken by the advancing penis. This causes some pain and often a little bleeding but the pain is likely to be worse if the muscles of the area are held taut through tension, fear or embarrassment. A truly caring husband will try to ease or allay this by a gentle and loving approach to his bride resulting in happy relaxation and expectancy. After a few times the vagina is sufficiently stretched for the whole of intercourse to be painless. Of course it is not just a mechanical act but part of a deep, loving communication between two people who, because of their love for each other, are more anxious to give than to receive joy and fulfilment.

Intercourse should be the culmination of the exploration and enjoyment of each other's body with abandonment to each other physically and emotionally. It should be a physical expression of union of mind and spirit in true love and can therefore be regarded as a sacrament of love.

We have stressed that sexual intercourse should never be seen as a physical act in isolation from the emotional and spiritual—if it is, it is debased. Apart from the fact that the body needs some preparation for the act to be fully satisfying, sexual union should be seen in the context of love and of physical and emotional closeness. This is achieved through prior love-play when, in a mood of relaxed enjoyment, each expresses their love in words, in caressing and stimulating the body of their partner, in kissing and embracing. There may be laughter, teasing and experimenting with what gives most enjoyment to the other, possibly including mock aggression. During such love-play, areas of the body which can produce sexual excitement are discovered and stimulated—for example, kissing the lips and other parts of the body, caressing the breasts and genitals, stroking the inner thighs, stroking the hair and so on. The stimulation and excitement produced prepares both for intercourse. In the husband this is achieved through erection of the penis and in the wife it leads to softening of the tissues around the vaginal entrance and secretion of a lubricant fluid to facilitate the penetration by the erect and enlarged penis. Such preparatory enjoyment can continue as long as the lovers wish, but usually before too long one or both need to proceed to intercourse to prevent an early climax or orgasm. The husband then inserts his penis into the entrance to the vagina and penetration into the vagina is achieved through a series of thrusting movements. This produces further intense sexual stimulus and pleasure in both partners who respond in rhythmic movements so that the wife's pelvic and vaginal muscles squeeze on the penis. Ultimately these movements spread throughout the bodies of both, intensifying their mutual embrace and feeling of oneness. The husband's climax or orgasm is reached with ejaculation or secretion of semen from the penis into the vagina and a feeling of great exhilaration, whilst the wife's reaction continues to her climax which is equally exciting and pleasurable. The climax of each further excites the other and sometimes—though not always—their orgasms coincide to the increased joy of both.

Failure to achieve a climax or adequate sexual response in one easily detracts from response in the other. This failure may be due to a number of causes many of which call for sensitivity. Sometimes the entrance to the vagina does not lubricate due to insufficient stimulation during love-play, straightforward tiredness or disinclination for some other reason. It is helpful, if the wife wants to continue, to smear on a bland jelly or cream (inquiries can be made from a doctor) and this can be done either by the wife herself or the husband. Lubrication can make a great difference in facilitating success and increasing response. A disturbing sound, fear of intrusion of privacy, pain, inner resentments, fears or guilt feelings can all interfere with or prevent sexual response. These may affect either partner, but perhaps more easily the woman.

Probably the most sensitive source of stimulation in a woman is the small penis-like organ called the clitoris. It is situated in the front of the vaginal entrance. When friction and pressure are exerted on the clitoris by the base of the penis during penetration and in subsequent movements there is a marked sexual response leading to orgasm. Knowing these facts, both partners can help each other and in particular the husband should not be content only with his own response but should persist in helping his wife to achieve her climax. Stimulation of the clitoris by the husband and the penis by the wife can be a helpful part of love-play.

It should not be expected that both partners will always achieve a full orgasm. Success in love-making should not be judged by this if it is seen in the context of the real relationship and communication which are embodied in the act. The more a couple strive for perfection or react to what they feel is failure, the less likely are they to find the fulfilment they seek and the more likely it is that tensions will arise through recriminations or a sense of guilt. The quality of love between two lovers is tested by their ability just to enjoy each other in relaxed mood and willingness to laugh together whilst giving as much as they can to each other. There has to be understanding in situations where one partner does not feel like making love. How does one convey to the other how they are feeling—that they want to make love or that they feel too tired or unwell to try? Ideally, couples should feel able to talk easily about their feelings, including what does or does not help them in love-play, or even what hurts them, without fear of the other taking offence. All too often couples find this difficult but they can learn to give and to receive signals which communicate what they want. If one is not feeling like intercourse the other should not interpret this as personal rejection. Sensitivity leads both to be content with just being close and achieving what intimacy both can easily cope with at that time. If this disinclination on the part of one happens too often, then it is important to talk about it to try to discover together what in their relationship may be producing these excuses. True love calls for honesty.

Following the climax of intercourse comes the stage of resolution when the penis goes limp again and both relax even though they may wish to remain as they are with the penis still in the vagina. There will be a feeling of weary contentment and often the couple will want to fall asleep in each other's arms. The desire for sleep is perhaps more common in the husband whilst the wife may be wide awake or even still excited. She needs her husband's continued embrace for a while before she settles happily. For the husband just to have his satisfaction and then simply turn over and go to sleep is to leave his wife feeling abandoned.

Prior to and during intercourse the position taken by husband and wife can vary according to their comfort and preference and what they find easiest for intercourse itself. In this, as in other aspects of their activities, couples should talk together to discover what each enjoys most and least. Marriage itself and sexual activities can so easily go stale without exploring and experimenting with different approaches, positions, ideas and techniques. It is surprising how often couples who are having problems have been denying themselves greater satisfaction and joy by not being able to talk about preferences and experimenting. A counsellor's role is often just to facilitate this communication and then relationships immediately improve.

Are there any rules?

Such guidance as has been given may be of help in avoiding mistakes and enriching the relationship of those happily married. We can of course be tied too much to the book like the wife who complained, 'I hate that book! When we are making love I know just when my husband gets to the bottom of page eight and starts on page nine. It's always the same and it makes me want to scream!'

There are no rules which say, for example, that love-making always has to take place in bed or at night. Any time of day or night anywhere is acceptable provided there is privacy and both want it that way. The key words are spontaneity and harmony and this applies whether the goal is the conception of a child or simply a way in which each communicates (that is what intercourse literally means) love to the other. Sadly it can become an exercise in self-gratification.

Couples vary greatly in how frequently they have intercourse. There are no rules. Again, the important thing is that the frequency should be mutually acceptable. There are marriages where the demands of the husband, for example, are greater than the wife can cope with and either she reluctantly acquiesces or resists and tension mounts. One partner may be constantly frustrated and feel neglected because the other's sexual needs are much less. Either way there is an element of selfishness or at least thoughtlessness and often a problem in communication. The ability to arrive at a frequency that keeps both happy is a measure of the quality of the relationship in general. The giving or withholding of sexual favours used as a weapon or means of getting one's own way is always destructive of a total relationship. The frequency tends to be greater in early marriage but it fluctuates throughout the marriage and often increases in later years when retirement comes and the stresses and strains of work and a growing family have gone. Incidentally, there is no upper age limit for sexual activity!

Some people ask what are the limits to variations in sexual play. Probably the answer for a happily married couple is that provided this comes naturally and *both* are happy with the activity, there are no limits.

Obviously there are no rules about how many children a couple should have. Before a Christian couple decides that they do not want any children (and there are no medical reasons for so deciding) they should sincerely search their hearts and talk together to discover if their motives are entirely consistent with Christian standards. The same applies to any decision about how many children to have, for they come as a sacred trust from God. Much unhappiness can arise and the relationship be seriously hurt if there is not agreement between a couple about the number of children they will have. Clearly, medical considerations with the advice of a doctor may come into the decision and issues like their joint Christian service and commitment have to be considered as does also finance, housing and many other factors. Unhappily, I have known Christian couples who have proved quite irresponsible, selfish and inconsiderate in their decisions, bringing no glory to God and often doing a serious disservice to their children and to each other. I have also known deception come into sexual relationships and contraceptive methods, even with Christian couples, so that one manipulates a pregnancy without the consent of the other. I have seen, years later, the disastrous result of one such selfish and deceptive act. The child conceived can continue to suffer through an unsatisfactory relationship with the parent who had not planned the conception, and of course the marriage relationship can be impaired for many years.

What is the meaning of sex?

All too often couples see intercourse as the only sexual expression of love in their relationship or see it as the all-important aspect of their relationship. It is interesting how quickly the niceties of courting days, when each was 'wooing' the other and on their best behaviour to impress, are lost after marriage when they have what they wanted! Even couples who have been married no longer than a year or two laugh sometimes when I ask them how long it is since they told their partner how much they love them. They think I am incurably romantic. Gone are the boxes of chocolates and bunches of flowers or even a pair of socks! Often it is rare for them to sit closely and hold hands whilst they relax, listen to music or enjoy anything together. The kiss when parting or returning has become a perfunctory token, if it occurs at all, whilst the closer physical contact like a cuddle hardly has a place in daily life. All of this is part of the total sexual relationship because these things are expressions of love between a man and woman in love. The effect upon children must also be considered for they feel secure when they *see* evidence of a loving bond between their parents and they need to grow up to feel at ease with their own sexuality.

Surprisingly often, couples wonder why they are not meeting with more success in their sexual activity in bed at the end of the day and see no connection with their 'sexual activities' or physical warmth and closeness during the day. After feverishly rushing around in their separate work during the day, each comes home to do their own thing during the evening. Husband may be snoozing behind his newspaper or book in one corner of the room whilst wife is busy in another corner or in the kitchen. Hardly a word passes between them or else tensions mount because of some disagreement. At a given time both retire to bed and wonder why their sexual performance is not exhilarating! All this is due to a total misunderstanding of the meaning of a sexual relationship. Most people cannot just switch off from the tensions, and even rows of a few moments ago, and give themselves completely to each other in sexual intercourse. Although this may affect the wife more, both are likely to be sensitive to these negative emotions which have an adverse effect on their sexual responses. It is true that there should be a healing and forgiving quality to sexual union which 'wipes the slate clean' but that is no substitute for talking through differences and by word and deed reducing tension. Intercourse then comes as the final seal upon reconciliation. A sincere 'I'm sorry' has to precede 'I love you, darling'. Nor is intercourse a satisfactory substitute for the acts of thoughtfulness, kindness and emotional and physical closeness that should be the hallmark of a loving relationship. Intercourse can be the culmination of all these.

Who makes the first move?

Many aspects of the sexual relationship between marriage partners have been considered—the expectations that each brings with them, what they convey or achieve through intercourse, the different techniques that may be used, the when, where and how, and the meaning their sexual life has for each, as well as the frequency of sexual union. The pattern which incorporates all these is unique for each couple. Again, it is not for anyone to lay down rules or suggest what is normal but often a change or adjustment can bring increased enrichment to their total marriage relationship.

Each couple also decides who takes the initiative in sexual advances. For a long time it was traditional that only the husband took the initiative and it was thought immodest if not improper for the wife to take the lead in any way. Her role was seen as submission as part of her wifely duties. In many cultures today this is still the recognised pattern but how does anyone else know what goes on in such intimate relationships, even when there is a strict cultural pattern which seeks to control instinctive human behaviour? But it is probably true to say that attitudes between husband and wife in marriage reflect the relative position of men and women in society in general. In most western societies men and women have equal standing and so it should be natural if husbands and wives each played their part in taking initiative in sexual relations. It would also seem logical that if each loved the other and sexual gestures are expressions of love then each would want spontaneously to tell the other how they felt. Intercourse itself allows each to make advances to the other if they wish but it is entirely their choice and there is no right or wrong. In every aspect of a loving relationship each would want to respect the other's rights and wishes and treat them as a unique, worthy individual with their own special feelings and needs in order to give them maximum happiness.

The honeymoon—fun or fiasco?

In anticipation, those first few days alone together after the wedding are emblazoned in romantic idealism, especially when the couple have deferred the deepest level of communication and sexual intimacy until they are husband and wife. The expectations for the honeymoon are often for perfect bliss and exhilarating sexual fulfilment. Sadly this is often not realised and, unless forewarned, lovers may become disillusioned and accusations or recriminations may follow. The key to enjoyment is a good sense of humour and fun, lots of patience and the ability to relax. The whole of married life lies ahead and there is plenty of time to achieve perfection. The honeymoon can be a time for a happy holiday alone and together in which each can just enjoy the other and begin to learn to live together at all levels. The learning may range from the experience of one bride I know who was shocked by the extraordinary noise her husband made when brushing his teeth—and when snoring—to the discovery of the attractiveness of each other's body and qualities of character. Hopefully, each discovers that they are even more in love with the one with whom they have chosen to spend the rest of their life.

Fidelity

When making our marriage vows we promise each other 'to love and to cherish till death us do part'. Marriage should be for life. We also promise to love, 'forsaking all others'. This special, close relationship has to be exclusive of any comparable relationship. Love at the depth implied within marriage cannot be shared. But we tend to equate faithfulness or fidelity with sexual fidelity and forget that it has much wider implications. To indulge in another sexual relationship outside of marriage can only debase the meaning of sex to both partners. But in our vows we promise to be faithful in many other aspects of our relationship—in love, in comfort, in honour and cherishing in good times and in bad. In addition, the salvationist couple promise to influence each other to seek the salvation of others which is a reminder that love is never selfish. Faithfulness in marriage is a commitment to God's holy estate of matrimony—the vocation of marriage itself. It is a vocation that joins two people together not only in the sight of God but in witness to man. Fidelity involves a commitment to the future of the marriage by ensuring that the relationship remains a living, growing experience of human love. This means a dedication to the other's happiness, well-being, and mental and spiritual growth, allowing areas of independence of personality and thought, yet at the same time becoming one in spirit. And so this has to be 'till death us do part'.

If the sexual relationship in a marriage is a deep level of communication physically, emotionally and spiritually, and intercourse is its culmination, then it must embody all these aspects of fidelity and, as already stated, it becomes a sacrament of love. Sexual intercourse can lead to the creation of life itself. Children born as a result are God's greatest gift and are a sacred trust requiring the care and nurture of a husband and wife in love. That love is in turn nurtured by the continuance of good sexual relationships and by the relationship of each partner with God. Love, more than anything else, provides the foundation of the personality and faith of the developing child.

Husband and wife share the privilege and responsibility of this most intimate of relationships and this calls for mutual trust and faithfulness. The rewards are very great in intense physical and emotional pleasure, in healing and renewal, in spiritual enrichment and in the happiness of the children.

5

Sexual difficulties

Dr and Mrs (Dr) Kildahl-Andersen (Norway)

*'So God created man in his own image, in the image of God
created he him; male and female created he them' (Genesis 1:27).*

*'Therefore shall a man leave his father and his mother, and shall
cleave unto his wife: and they shall be one flesh' (Genesis 2:24).*

THUS begins the history of mankind, and thus begins the history
of marriage. In other words, marriage is a covenant where two
different and independent individuals function in an intimate
fellowship in both good and bad days. It is not to be wondered at
that this does not always happen without a hitch and without
problems! And even for those who have a good harmonious
marriage sexually, there can be occasions when it is easy for sexual
tensions to arise. The last chapter dealt with difficulties in the early
months of marriage; this chapter deals with problems arising later.

Pregnancy and childbirth

During the last period of pregnancy intercourse is both
technically difficult and inadvisable. During this phase the woman
is occupied with the child and has little need for sex. For the man,
the need is the same as before and the long period of sexual
restraint can be a pressure.

Then the birth is over and maybe he thinks, 'At last we can be
together again.' However, he finds that his wife has absolutely no
interest in sex—not for weeks or months, perhaps many months.
The woman has changed psychologically. There are both
anatomical and hormone changes. She is tired and weary, has a
child with whom she is occupied day and night and her husband
comes second. In some instances the husband feels 'out of it' and
becomes rather jealous of the child. Behind this rejection on the
woman's part can lie the fear of a new pregnancy.

In short, there are many factors during this period which can cause pressure on the marriage. Here the husband must exercise great patience and not go brutally ahead, but rather allow his wife to decide the pace. In the majority of cases all will be normal again in the course of a few weeks or months. Here, as always, there should be complete frankness and understanding between partners.

There are usually courses on pregnancy, birth and child-care for both mothers-to-be and fathers-to-be. It is important to have practical information regarding the circumstances which make for difficulties after birth. The husband should know that it is natural and normal for the wife to react in such a way after the birth, and they must seek to help and support each other during this period which puts pressure on both partners, albeit in different ways.

The menopause

Another chapter in life where it is natural for problems to arise is in connection with the woman's menopause. With intercourse as a function for reproduction it is natural that there should be a point at which to stop such activity. However, it is not so simple. For the harmonious couple, intercourse is a means of joy and an expression of love for each other and a strengthening of fellowship and togetherness, and as such it can naturally continue.

During this period there are psychological, physical, hormone and secretion changes in a woman which cause a decline in her need for sex. The ability to accomplish the sexual act may also be reduced whilst the man may still have a considerable need for sex. One can find examples of men who are driven to adultery during this period simply because of the wife's rejection, sexually. But fortunately, this is the exception. The majority can manage to adapt to each other and continue with a normal sex life even during this period and right through to old age. The differences between individuals with regard to need and practice are great.

Illness

Up to now mention has been made of periods in the marriage when it is natural for sexual tensions to arise. Now we turn to situations where one partner is overtaken by illness of one kind or another. It is obvious that illness or surgery affecting the sex organs either temporarily or permanently can put a stop to a normal sex life. The same can also apply to a greater or lesser degree with an illness affecting movement, such as paralysis, arthritis and so on.

A little less obvious, there are illnesses which, though they do not affect any particular organ of the body, nevertheless lead to a general weakness in one's condition and can lead to impotence and reduced sexual need for a shorter or longer duration. The same can arise during periods of psychological problems, depression or special stress situations. It is not always easy for the healthy person, rarely or never ill, to enter into, understand or accept the illness of the other partner. Lack of understanding of a marriage partner who neither physically nor psychologically feels able to carry on a normal sex life increases the pain and leads to conflict and mistrust. If such problems arise it is important for both partners to find a simpler way to show tenderness and love for each other. There is an old saying: '*Love begets love.*'

One situation which should also be mentioned in this connection and which, perhaps, is not so well known, is the effect that different medicines can have upon the sex life. The sexual function is a complicated exercise made up of many factors. It is not so strange, therefore, that medication can have its influence. It can affect various mechanisms—and there are various types of medicine one could mention, for example: certain blood pressure pills, some hormone preparations, medicines used for psychological suffering. The effect can be partly dependent on the dosage. The majority of these affect the sexual function by reducing libido (desire for sex), causing impotence or preventing an erection. Should the problem occur where one partner is dependent upon long-term medication, they should seek advice from a doctor. If it is thought that the medicine itself is the cause of the problem, then in many instances it could probably be changed for something else.

When illness or other problems hinder the natural sex life it can be a test for the marriage. What is it that binds the two together? Is it sex, or a genuine love which holds out and withstands all, come what may? It may be that when trials come a spouse realises the other's true worth as a human being and as a life-partner. Then their intercourse can give new surprises and enrichment. Unfortunately however, some circumstances can lead to adultery.

Adultery

Adultery is a word which is sometimes taboo, but we know that it exists and we must therefore be frank about it. By adultery we mean a relationship between a married man or married woman with someone who is not their marriage partner. In our day it is still regarded as serious. In Norway, for example, it is still a ground for immediate divorce without a period of separation, although laws vary from country to country.

The causes of adultery are varied. There are frequent occurrences of sexual incompatibility between married couples. Usually this incompatibility has existed from the beginning of their life together. Both partners have, in a way, accepted this but the habitual routine has completely destroyed the sex life of the marriage partners. Other more practical circumstances can lead to adultery. The wife becomes weary through housework, childbirth or child care, with little rest. On the other hand the husband works hard in his job. She rejects him simply because she is worn out and cannot produce the energy a healthy sex life requires. In addition, she may sometimes have a desire for revenge, a desire to 'punish' him or humiliate him because she is at home all the time whilst he is out and occupied elsewhere 'doing his own thing'.

He, for his part, will feel rejected and when he meets another woman he begins a relationship with her. He is completely frustrated at home—but it is highly doubtful that his frustration will lessen with this new relationship.

However, even when there is a good relationship within the marriage, adultery sometimes takes place. These, however, are usually single episodes and need not completely destroy the marriage. But when adultery is a reaction due to marital conflicts and sexual frustration, the infidelity will often be long-term and lead to a break-up of the marriage.

In some cases adultery may be the outcome of a need for variation. There is a philosophical viewpoint, not held by everyone and certainly not held by Christians, that when a man loves a woman, he loves all women, or, at least, is capable of so doing. Now and then a man or woman is temporarily infatuated with a third person. In such instances a man will often commit 'psychic' adultery—that is, he will dream and fantasise on how the other person performs sexually (Jesus warned of this in Matthew 5:28). If under such circumstances a man really does commit adultery, it may be an expression of his desire for adventure and excitement.

Finally, it must also be mentioned that lack of sexual fulfilment is another important factor which leads to infidelity. The reason may be physical or psychological conflicts, or simply unequal sexual desires in the partner. Usually, adultery causes even further conflict and nervous pressure for those involved. Frustration which was bad enough before only gets worse. One becomes caught in an ever-tightening net. Guilt crowds in.

When one married partner—more often the man—enters a homosexual relationship with a third person this is extremely serious (see below). For the wife it will seem like double infidelity—

43

first and foremost to her and then towards the female sex as a whole.

When adultery is committed, the discovery by the partner comes as a shock which casts an enormously dark shadow over the marriage. Sometimes the discovery will confirm the insecurity and perhaps the suspicion felt for a long time.

What can be done to help such a situation? There is no simple rule. No two marriages are alike, just as no two people are alike. People react differently to similar problems and challenges. As Christians we must regard adultery as inconsistent with God's will and therefore as sin. But there are no grounds to indicate that this sin cannot be pardoned by God—as with other sins.

As co-workers with God, we must not over-dramatise an incident of adultery. For the marriage partners it is often dramatic enough as it is. When the question of blame arises it is often impossible to say who is at fault. When we consider the various causes we have mentioned, the actual question of blame may not arise. As a counsellor it is impossible to take sides. Yet to know the cause of the adultery is essential and this should be the object of examination by both parties.

Should the love between the marriage partners be completely dead, the infidelity on top of everything else will most likely lead to a break-up of the marriage. But in most cases one instance of adultery need not end with a separation.

If we, as Salvation Army soldiers, temper our reaction to a case of adultery, allowing those to judge the case who are authorised to do so, whilst we surround those implicated with an unbroken chain of prayer, much will be achieved. We believe that the best solution is when God comes to those involved with his transforming power and renewal in thought, word and deed.

Homosexuality

It is claimed that 10 to 20 per cent of all men are bi-sexual or homosexual and that 40 per cent have had sexual experience with other men, usually in their teens but not thereafter. The percentage for women is a good deal lower. And, although a practising homosexual cannot be admitted to soldiership in the Army, we must reckon with the fact that there are a number of latent homosexuals and lesbians within our ranks. Our response to these folk will be Christlike. They will often need sensitive, well-informed pastoral care.

We have clear authority to hold on to, namely, the word of God. Homosexual practices are not an unknown phenomenon in

44

Scripture. They are condemned both in the Old and the New Testaments: Leviticus 18:22, 20:13; 1 Corinthians 6:9; Romans 1:27.

A number of church communities, like the Army, have taken the view that a homosexual *orientation* is not blameworthy, but that homosexual *conduct* is not permitted for a Christian. What is meant by 'practices' is not usually defined. A homosexual orientation may often, though not inevitably so, lead to homosexual practices of one form or another—either psychic (thoughts, dreams, fantasies) or physical (sexual stimulation with others of the same sex, a relationship of short or long duration). It is the latter which Scripture expressly prohibits, whilst *all* impure thoughts require the purifying power of Christ.

The picture men had in former days of homosexuals as pale, effeminate, depressed, neurotic men, is not typical. They can look the same as heterosexuals and, in the main, succeed as well in life as others. In fact, it is well known that many famous men have been homosexuals.

Homosexuals and lesbians who have been converted to Christ often witness to the fact that they have been freed from these tendencies. Christian homosexuals who see such tendencies as a problem can experience the same. We mean therefore that the only solution for homosexuals is for them to experience release from homosexual tendencies and practices through the power of God. A number of homosexuals are married and for such the problems are even greater; again, the only possible release is for God to take control of their lives.

Some people, especially women who are good friends and work well together, find it practical and convenient to live together. They are often exposed to criticism and are also exposed to temptation. But to live under the same roof is not tantamount to sharing a bed. Good friendship is not the same as homosexuality, and one would warn against regarding all such associations with suspicion.

Pornography

In the wake of deviations and sexual perversion an enormous pornographic industry has developed in some countries. Hard pornography portrays not only the normal positions for intercourse, but speculates on all kinds of sexual conduct, performing with persons of the same sex, with children, with implements, sometimes with violence, and even with animals. More serious still is the fact that soft pornographic pictures and indecent writings are creeping into the more accepted weekly magazines and newspapers, together with violence in films and television—and there is a danger of our becoming accustomed to and accepting it passively.

Behind all this stands an enormous industry out to make great profits. Pornography and so-called erotic art can be an effective stimulant through commercial advertising. Pornography is not only soul-destroying, it is also very costly. It is a degradation of womanhood and an insult to human sexuality which is a lovely and sacred gift from God. In pornography men force women to comply with their wishes obediently and passively, to bring gratification to the man.

In the ranks of Christians and far beyond there is a growing hostility towards pornography, for it often creates serious sexual problems. It makes problems between individual spouses in that expectations are raised artificially and one spouse, usually the husband, may make intolerable demands on the other on the basis of what has been seen in the pornographic literature or film. The presence of pornography in the home can easily destroy a wife's sexual appetite. It encourages reliance on artificial sex and may even lead to an inability to form a normal sexual relationship with a real partner.

The Army's viewpoint regarding pornographic literature and films has always been clear and there are absolutely no grounds to change this attitude today. We must not be led astray by the news and statistics which claim that sexual crimes have decreased a little in countries where pornography is freely accessible. The explanation for this lies in the liberalisation of the law. Fewer people will be punished for sexual offences because certain actions will no longer be regarded as crimes. Other personal tragedies are, without doubt, on the increase in the same countries. Our emotional life has not been helped by the increasing liberality.

Our world abounds with sexual perversions and temptations. Some individuals will suffer shipwreck as they sail their vessel in such unclean waters. But here are four basic principles:

1 First and foremost we must ensure that our conduct is right—that we have a harmonious relationship with our marriage partner and that we keep from us all unclean thoughts, words and actions.
2 If we are to be successful in our community life we must have order in our private life—10 years in the medical profession and as counsellors have taught us this.
3 God's word is a sure guide for all humanity and only by upholding this truth can we have an influence on those around us, and thus reverse the present trend.
4 There is no remedy to be found for all the evil in the world other than to cast oneself upon the Lord Jesus Christ and to live under his control.

6

Family planning

Mrs Captain (Dr) Pat Hill (New Zealand)

TO many couples becoming parents is a natural consequence of being married. Julie and Rod plan to get married. Julie has a well-paid job as a secretary and Rod is a motor mechanic. They have saved for years and are now ready to raise loans to enable them to buy a home. Julie wants an old house which they can renovate themselves in their spare time. Rod aims for a new house on a new housing estate. Reluctantly Julie is coming round to his way of thinking although she knows that in order to afford this she will have to work for at least three more years after marriage before starting a family. She has mixed feelings about this.

A pattern has emerged in western society. People get married, then set up a home and later start a family. How different from Julie's and Rod's grandparents' day, when young people got married and usually before a year was passed the first baby had arrived.

Childlessness by choice

These days there is a choice. Couples do not have to become parents if they do not want to. There are many reasons why people choose not to have children. For example:

'We were content in our relationship and did not want an intruder.'
'We both had careers with good prospects and were happy and did not want children.'
'With the state of the world as it is, who would want to bring children into it?'
'I don't really like children.'
'We really wanted to be free to do our own thing.'

There are still powerful pressures, social and emotional, for couples to have children, but in some cultures these are less than they were a generation ago. People have a right to choose whether or not they want to be parents.

47

Childlessness not by choice

If, after a year without contraception, the wife has not conceived and the couple do want children, they should seek medical advice. Infertility is not just one partner's problem. Two individuals' systems must work correctly before they can successfully conceive a child, so both partners should be seen by the doctor.

If there is no hope of conceiving a child, couples may consider alternatives. These days there are fewer children available for adoption than there were a few years ago. This means that few couples will have the opportunity to adopt. If they want to adopt, certain questions must be answered. Do they want to know and keep in contact with the birth parents? Would they be prepared to adopt a child of another race? Would they consider adopting an older child? Could they take a child with a handicap?

There is a great need for informed couples to take the risk and help children in need of fostering, children who may have a disturbed background. This is often a temporary relationship, and can be difficult for the couple to handle.

For many couples adoption or fostering are not possible and reluctantly they have to accept that they will remain childless. For many this is a painful adjustment which can either embitter or enrich their marriage.

Having to get married

Mary and Joe had been 'going steady' for two years. Last June, Mary realised that she was pregnant. Because of family pressure they decided to get married immediately.

Many couples marry because a baby is on the way. This often puts a great strain on a new marriage relationship. Many questions need to be faced. Would the couple have married if pregnancy had not made it necessary? Can the shame and guilt be worked through? Is it the couple's own wish or their parents' wish that they marry? Are the couple prepared for parenthood? How economically viable is this prospective family unit? Are there extended family and friends who will support the couple if they do decide to marry?

It is certainly advisable to wait until marriage to have intercourse and children. It is not always a disaster for a couple to 'have to get married', but it takes a strong couple to hold together in this situation.

Planning a family

Julie and Rod decided not to have a family until the second mortgage was paid off. They both went to the doctor, who advised them four months before their marriage that Julie should start on the pill. Julie stayed on the pill for the next three years. She stopped it in November and conceived the following May.

Contraception can be discussed with your doctor or at a family planning clinic. If you are engaged, don't wait until a week before the marriage to get advice. Go some months before marriage to find out what methods are available and decide what suits you as a couple. You may still decide to change this later on.

How contraception works

A woman's reproductive cycle usually takes place in 28-day periods. On the first day of her period she begins to bleed as she loses the lining of her womb. This will last for three or four days. After this the lining of her womb thickens again and an egg ripens in her ovary. In the middle of her 28-day cycle (ie on day 14) the egg is released from the ovary. Evidence that this has happened can be a rise in her temperature, and the mucus from her womb is clear and stringy. The egg travels along a tube towards the womb. If it meets a sperm from the male while travelling along this tube the egg and sperm will unite and the egg will become fertilised. The fertilised egg travels to the womb, the lining of which has become thick and juicy to receive it. It burrows into the lining (implantation) and a baby begins to develop.

If a fertilisation has not taken place however, the thick lining of the womb breaks up and the woman's period begins. One cycle has been completed and the next one commences.

In the male, sperms form in the testes and travel in their millions up the tubes and out through the penis. With sexual excitement the penis becomes hard and erect; if it is inserted into the woman's vagina the sperms are deposited there and travel up to meet the egg should one be released from the ovaries. It takes only one sperm to fertilise an egg and create a baby.

All forms of contraception try to stop the egg in the female from meeting a sperm from the male.

Types of contraception available

1 Barriers to sperm meeting the egg

(a) *Condoms* are the only contraceptives available for men to use. A condom is a thin rubber sheath with a space at the end of the tube to catch the sperm. It is put on over an erect penis and is sometimes used with foams or jellies which will kill the sperm and aid lubrication. The advantages are that they are cheap, can be bought without a prescription and will protect against venereal disease.

However, some men feel that it reduces the sensation for them, and they have to remember to apply them before having intercourse. They have a 95 per cent success rate in preventing pregnancy.

(b) *A diaphragm* is a rubber cap which fits over the opening to the womb, called the cervix. It has to be fitted to ensure that it is the right size for the woman's cervix and it is inserted before going to bed at night and left in until morning. It is used with spermicidal creams. It has a 90 per cent success rate in preventing pregnancy.

(c) *Spermicidal jellies* can be applied to the penis and vagina to kill the sperm. They have a less than 90 per cent chance of preventing a pregnancy if used just on their own.

2 Methods to stop egg production

(a) The 'pill' is an oral contraceptive for women containing two hormone-like substances which prevent pregnancy mainly by stopping the monthly release of an egg cell from the ovary. Whilst she is taking the pill regularly her hormones are not produced. If she stops taking the pill her hormones take over again and she could become pregnant. If a woman experiences side effects from it she should contact a doctor immediately. There are many brands and a suitable type can often be found. It is almost 100 per cent reliable if taken according to directions and many women find their periods are less painful and shorter and that pre-menstrual tension is less.

(b) *The Depoprovera injection* can be given every three months. Usually the woman will not bleed at all while on this. Side effects are fluid retention, an increased incidence in breast lumps and a slow return to fertility. It is unproven that Depoprovera causes cancer.

3 Mechanical interference

To stop the fertilised egg being implanted in the woman a device (for example, a coil) is put into the uterus. The advantage is that there is no hormonal upset, and the woman does not have to remember to do anything before intercourse or to take a pill every day. Disadvantages are an increase in bleeding and a slight risk of pregnancy occurring outside the uterus.

4 Natural family planning or periodic abstinence

For this method to work a woman has to have a regular cycle and to know when she ovulates. Intercourse is avoided when she is potentially fertile. Psychologically this can be unsatisfactory and is an unreliable method for most.

5 Sterilisation

This is when the tubes in the female are cut and tied so that the eggs cannot pass down the tubes. The male counterpart is vasectomy when the tubes in the male are cut and tied to prevent sperm passing out of the penis. This is a sure way to prevent pregnancy, but these processes are seldom reversible if either partner should ever remarry and want another child.

6 Coitus interruptus

This is when the penis is removed from the vagina just before the sperms are to be released in ejaculation. It is an unreliable and unsatisfactory method.

From the variety of contraceptive methods available a couple can choose what suits them, and change to another method if the need arises.

Cultural variations in contraception

What may be acceptable in a western culture, elsewhere may be quite unacceptable or at least viewed with suspicion. In many developing countries it is often difficult to persuade couples to limit the number of children because they 'accept what God gives us' and they need to be sure those children they do have will survive to adulthood so they can help to support their parents in old age: especially where there is no social security system. For many the status of parents still varies directly with the number of children they have. However, in many such cultures the over-population problem is so serious that efforts should be made to help couples to accept the importance of limiting the size of their families, though without at the same time offending sincerely held beliefs. Smaller families may not only relieve them of abject poverty and starvation but also safeguard the health, and even the life, of mother and wife. Further, reducing the birth-rate is of vital importance to a developing nation as a whole. Often the mothers are fairly convinced of the value of smaller families but the fathers are reluctant to accept the same view. Patient teaching and explanation is therefore required for fathers as well as mothers. In the end, of course, the decision about when to conceive and how many children to have belongs to each couple. There is a trend for the number of children per family to decrease as the level of education and general standard of living in a society improves. Amongst the less-educated and developed people it is important that a simple method of contraception is recommended, for example, condoms or three-monthly Depoprovera injections from a clinic.

51

From spouse to parent

Julie and Rod had a son. After all the celebrations, the responsibility of being parents really hit them when Julie brought the baby home. Julie became weepy and irritable; the baby was a poor sleeper and cried for hours on end. Rod was glad to escape to work each day. Fortunately, Julie's parents saw what was happening and helped Julie and Rod through this difficult time.

Helen and Robert had a baby within a year of marriage. Robert was delighted to see Helen so happy but gradually he became resentful of the baby. Was he jealous of his own son? The boy took up so much of Helen's time and she wouldn't let him help. Robert felt left out.

Joy and Peter had a daughter. Peter was so delighted that he wanted to stay at home with his wife and baby—work was an intrusion. He felt an overwhelming sense of privilege in being a parent.

The coming of the first baby

We often prepare ourselves better for marriage than we do for parenthood. When we feel an overwhelming nurturing instinct rise within us as we hold in our arms our own innocent, helpless baby, we think parenting will come naturally. To some it does but, however enthusiastic we are, it often takes time and experience to learn to develop a strong bond with our child and at the same time maintain ourselves as parents and as a couple. Most parents feel anxious at first with a new baby. A mother may feel that 'up to now my body was doing all the nurturing of the baby but now it is over to me'. These demanding initial weeks—or months, or years—can make or mar a marriage.

As the primary care-giver, the mother has great demands placed upon her in caring for the child. Initially, she can be emotional, nervous, weepy, tire easily, and she needs her husband's understanding. It has been said, 'Give me a good mother and I shall make a better world.' Can we say, 'Give me a good father and we shall have a good mother'? Women need men to make the job of mothering easier, more fulfilling and, at times, even tolerable.

Parenting is a shared responsibility. Nature will make a mother of a wife, but it often takes a wife to make a husband a father. The transition from lovers, friends or partners to parents is neither simple nor smooth. For the first time there is competition from another deep, attractive relationship. Helen shut Robert out, and no wonder he felt jealous of his own child! How easy it would be for Robert to go out and find his consolation elsewhere! If a woman can communicate, say how she feels to her husband and get him to help in the care of the child, both will form stronger bonds with each other and with the child. Having an active role in the home and with his children, does not diminish a man's masculinity. He knows his children, understands their development and character and behaviour; his opinions carry weight and his judgments respect. Tenderness and gentleness are as important in a man in his family as are courage and strength.

Having made it through the first year of parenting, we can see a lot of the tensions in better perspective. We are better able to find a balance in our own and other people's expectations of us as parents. We may not be the ideal parents—we may not have the ideal child—but we know that we are able to cope and survive both as a couple and as parents.

Just as the child needs to be nurtured, so do parents. Rod and Julie had an extended family and friends who supported them and helped them to support each other. With the increasing mobility of families, some couples may be without close family or friends nearby when the baby comes. As a couple they may have to seek support from, for example, parent support groups. As Christians, we should be on the lookout for stress in new parents in our neighbourhood.

Parenthood as stewardship

It has been said that we do not appreciate our own parents until we are parents ourselves. Some are 'born parents', but most of us have to learn by trial and error the art of being a parent. It will help us in this task if we remember that our children are a gift, on trust, from God. They are not ours to keep but ours to encourage to grow to maturity—physically, emotionally and spiritually. Who is equal to such a task? How we need the support of each other in coping with each stage of their development, and resolving any conflicts and tensions which may arise as two different adults deal with the same child! We have to learn which of our needs we can expect to have met, and which ones have to be shelved until our children are older. We have to learn to live within the restrictions of parenthood and cope with the continuing commitment and responsibility.

With God's help we can learn to balance our own needs with those of our children and our partners. Parenthood means an end to self-pleasing as a couple and the beginning of self-denying service; with this can come a sense of completeness and great joy.

7

Communicating

Mrs Margaret Mead (South Africa)

MARRIAGE is not so much *finding* the right person as it is *being* the right person (Charlie W. Shedd). Communication in marriage is not something that just happens, it needs to be worked at and prayed over. Since marriage involves a series of decisions, communication is extremely important.

The origin of a communication problem often goes right back to the courting days. Sometimes young people go on dates only for the sake of going out, rather than from common interests. Occasionally this sort of relationship drifts into marriage, and although communication is not a strong point, the other party erroneously thinks, 'I'll change that after we're married'. It is a fact that even fairly talkative people sometimes become uncommunicative after marriage; so there is very little hope for those whose communication lacks something even at this early stage, unless this is dealt with in a prayerful and God-inspired way.

There are some good guidelines for keeping the communication channels open in marriage. Try these 11 commandments:

1 Spend sufficient time together to give plenty of opportunity for open lines of communication. Failure in this is actually the main reason why communication dries up. So much time is spent on work, hobbies and so on that the partners become extremely tired. One recommendation here is that the couple go away alone together for a weekend or longer at least once every six months. This might not always be easy to arrange, but for the sake of the marriage it should be done. So often men have been heard to say that their secretary understands them better than their wife does. This is not really surprising, considering how much time a secretary can spend with her boss.

2 Concentrate fully on what your partner is saying during conversation. Listening with half an ear is just like not hearing at all. Eye contact is extremely important. Face each other while

54

conversing. Having one's head in a newspaper, or sewing, is not conducive to good communication!

3 Don't interrupt. Give your partner a chance to finish what he or she is saying. Also, try not to correct him or her in public, especially in a derogatory manner.

4 Respect sensitive areas. Tenderness is needed here. Recognise them and try to build up instead of breaking down. Remember that Satan breaks down, but Christ builds up.

5 Discuss problems as they happen or as soon after as possible. Don't let them simmer—they just *grow*! Failure to work through inevitable difficulties causes future problems.

6 Recognise that touch is important in communication, sometimes without words; tenderness is required.

7 Speak the truth in love. 'Use . . . helpful words, the kind that build up and provide what is needed, so that what you say will do good to those who hear you' (Ephesians 4:29, *Good New Bible*). Don't be afraid to reveal your weaknesses or inmost desires; and don't come unglued if your partner tells you a few home truths you don't like! This is progress!

8 Don't be self-centred. Selfishness is often a great stumbling block in marriage. It is part of our human nature, but in a good marriage it is kept under control. Give your partner time to express his or her opinions and desires. Don't dominate the conversation as this causes frustration; and try to see the other's point of view.

9 Express your appreciation of one another, with special reference to the areas usually taken for granted, for instance, going to work daily, cooking, personal appearances, driving, conscientiousness and so on. Admire each other often and verbally. This builds up a person's self-image. Don't confuse flattery with genuine appreciation.

10 Respect confidences shared with you. Repeating confidences is the quickest way to destroy trust in a relationship; and without trust, communication breaks down completely.

11 Know when to stop. Don't dig up bones of contention! Don't dwell on past history, but build a better future—together.

Apologising

Knowing how to apologise plays a very important part in communication. Some people find it very difficult to do. Often our partner's reaction to our apology has a great deal to do with our attitude to it. We should check this in ourselves. Are our retorts to an apology in this vein: 'It's about time' or 'I should think so' or something similar? Perhaps we are directly responsible for our spouse's reluctance to apologise.

We should silently examine our quarrels for tell-tale signs of whether or not we are the guilty party—at least to some extent.

We should be careful to use the right words when apologising. A little less of 'I'm sorry', which is used so flippantly at times, and more of 'I was wrong', which claims responsibility for action, would help. Bigness may never start unless it starts in us. Even if it is *all* your partner's fault, which is unlikely, you can still patch up a quarrel and yet keep your self-respect. Even when your spouse refuses to be honest, you can say, 'I'm sorry we argued. Please forgive me for anything I shouldn't have said.' Make sure your partner realises that his or her love is very important to you, and that when you are out of sorts with each other it really hurts you. When a couple are each prepared to go more than half-way to find harmony, then the relationship has a good chance of being successful.

Humour is a great diffuser of tension. Use it as often as you can; when times are good, or not so good. Don't be afraid to laugh at yourself.

Try to ask yourself not whose fault it is or why, but 'how best can I remedy the situation?'

Give and take

It goes without saying that this is a vital aspect of marriage. If it is missing, the relationship deteriorates into that of master and servant, and there is very little real sharing.

The human tendency is to be selfish, and taking comes naturally to many, but giving is an art to be learned and in the long run produces far more pleasure than receiving. Of course, with giving there must be a taker, and accepting love or gifts involves pride. So, much joy will be lost to the giver if the person receiving does not do so graciously. Have you ever chosen a gift specially for someone, anticipating a glad reaction, only to find that when you presented your gift it was ignored or put on one side to be opened at a later stage? What an anti-climax! Most of the pleasure in giving rests on the reaction of the recipient to the choice of gift. Have you ever been guilty here? Some people rush to change the gift with very little sensitivity towards the feelings of the giver. There are ways to do this and ways definitely not to do it.

Sometimes compassion is mistaken for pity, and a gesture of giving, whether a gift or something less tangible, like help, is either rejected or accepted ungraciously. Perhaps we should check up on ourselves in this area too. Are we too proud to accept help or kindness?

Giving requires special comment too. We must be alert to situations around us, particularly in our own home, where we can alleviate a problem or smooth the path a bit. Are we aware of what is needed around us? Just a word here and there can be a clue to a much greater need. Do we keep our eyes and ears open to notice what is really needed and choose our 'gift' accordingly? Do we notice areas where our help could be acceptable? We should also be careful not to intrude by an insensitive approach, so that what we do or give is easier to accept.

Compromise

Compromise is finding a middle road between two extremes, and is often necessary in marriage. A stubborn and rebellious nature can kill the art of compromise in a marriage. People who always insist on and get their own way become tyrants and are very difficult to live with. In the process something detrimental happens to the other person's feeling of self-worth; so it is very destructive. Communication plays an important part here as, if the feelings are not brought out into the open, the situation deteriorates and is much more difficult to correct.

Compromise in this context does not mean a lowering of standards to keep the peace, but involves communication at a deep level—the finding of common ground where both spouses feel comfortable.

Rigidity and lack of co-operation—which are selfishness in the extreme—do not enable a couple to find the happy medium between the two extremes. This takes time and effort, and a loving and caring attitude is imperative. Our attitudes are responsible for most of our wrong behaviour.

To show consideration in marriage involves a lack of selfishness and an understanding of the opposite sex. Men and women have always been different—that's how they are designed. A concerted effort is needed in stress situations to understand how the other thinks and the other's priorities. There are many helpful books available which will help you to understand what makes your partner tick. (See the useful reading list in the appendices.)

Misunderstandings so often occur through different interpretations or emphasis on ordinary words. Take the word 'tired' for instance. When a man says he is tired he usually means he wants to relax with his feet up, have an early night or at least do as little as possible. When a woman (particularly a housewife) says she is tired, she could easily mean that she is 'sick and tired' of staying at home, cleaning the house or doing humdrum things, and would love a change of scenery, an opportunity to do something more exciting or at least different, to break the monotony. She can almost always find the energy to go shopping for a new dress or to enjoy a good dinner out at a restaurant or some other form of entertainment. Misunderstanding can be due entirely to different interpretations of words.

Married people are often guilty of another misunderstanding—the sin of assumption. We are too quick to assume that our partner will behave in a particular way, and when we find we are wrong in our assumption, the natural reaction is to lash out (usually with our tongue) and berate our partner for lack of consideration. What has really happened is that he or she has not reacted in what we consider to be the normal way (which is probably something near to the way our family or we ourselves would react). Different backgrounds and experiences cause different people to behave in different ways. So we are not in a position to judge somebody else, even if it is our wife or husband, because we cannot get inside their head and think exactly like they think. It is good to make allowances for discrepancies in this type of situation.

Essentially though, compromise cannot be achieved without sincere and open communication between the spouses. The love of God needs to flow through you to your husband or wife—just human love alone cannot achieve a lasting result.

Accepting our partner and children exactly as they are, and not trying to push them into a mould we feel would be better for them, is important in the extreme. It is good to remember that we too have weaknesses and we expect to be accepted just as we are. You know God made your loved one with just the same precision as he made you, and after all you chose her or him, didn't you? God accepts you as you are, and we should try to do the same. He accepts us in this way so that we can become what he wants us to be. We should get our hands off, and allow God to do any moulding that is needed.

It is good to remember when we talk about loving our neighbour as ourself, that our partner and our children are our closest neighbours.

Relaxing

To become truly a couple requires the breaking down of protective (but obstructive) walls around ourselves. This takes time and can also be painful, but is a very important step towards oneness. It is partly finding out what makes the other one tick, and being sensitive to what makes him or her comfortable.

A man in particular seems often to wear a mask in his work situation. He has to conform to what is required of him there and to fit into that particular mould for certain hours a day, just to earn a decent living. It is crucial for him to be able to relax and be himself at home. Home should be the place where he can remove any facade and 'let his hair down'. If he doesn't feel really comfortable at home, either because it's too impeccable or for some other reason, he will be inclined to gravitate towards a place where he *can* unwind—whether it be with the 'boys' or wherever—and his home ties will weaken.

This seems rather an awesome responsibility for the wife, but it is widely agreed that the woman sets the tone of the home, and not only is she usually the creative one as regards the material aspects of the home, but the atmosphere is also largely formed by her.

Finance

In the area of finance there is a potential for disagreement, if not explosion! Budgeting is important, and should be a joint venture. It is important for the partners to have a good idea of the expenses necessarily incurred in the function of their spouse's role in the marriage. It is a good plan for the couple to go shopping together occasionally, as this helps to keep the husband, in particular, in touch with inflation and the effect it has on the housekeeping allowance. The reverse is also true, in that not every wife has a good idea of what a smart suit costs, for instance.

A good balance is required between what is needed and what is desired. Don't try to keep up with anyone else, but live within your limits. It is a mistake to try and insist on or demand more than your spouse is capable of. Remember that love covers a multitude of sins, and a loving approach and response in this type of situation is the only way to handle it. It is far better to talk about the problems and work together to sort them out. And don't harp on past offences—this is most destructive.

It is important for the wife to have some money she can call her own—not necessarily a large amount—but something that is essentially hers. Whether it is an allowance for her personal use—over and above the housekeeping money—or a savings account which she can build up or draw on without reference to her husband, doesn't really matter, but it is important for her self-image. There's nothing more humiliating than for a woman to have to ask her husband for money to buy him a gift for his birthday, or more complex than trying to get money out of him for a surprise (?) party. It makes her feel 'owned'.

There must be a certain amount of freedom in this area if at all possible, as too many rigid restrictions cause a feeling of claustrophobia in the relationship. The main criterion here, once again, is communication. Be solution-minded, and stop focusing on the problem. There is a way out of this sort of problem. Commit your finances and yourselves to the Lord, and allow him to take control.

Before we leave the subject of finance, just a short reminder that our financial planning will work out a good deal better if we give the Lord his share. You'll find that your 90 per cent of your income will go much further than 100 per cent will. After all, the Bible promises that 'God shall supply all your need according to his riches in glory by Christ Jesus' (Philippians 4:19).

Happy ever after?
Professor Lee Fisher (USA)

THERE are differences of opinion about the belief that 'marriages are made in Heaven'. In a marriage between Christians it is my conviction that, regardless of the circumstances that bring people together, it is necessary for the assurance of God's blessing to be experienced through the 'witness of the Spirit'. In this sense, a Christian marriage always involves a spiritual dimension that originates in Heaven. When a person accepts this, however, there is the danger of believing that all that happens 'ever after' is God's responsibility! Those Christians who have some understanding of married life know that, although divine approval is needed, marriage is lived out on earth. It involves differences in judgment, conflicts of feelings, variations in goals, and many other human characteristics that must be worked out in the give-and-take of everyday living.

Any relationship that demands total commitment involves risks. Inherent in the great challenges of life are the possibilities that something may go wrong and corrective measures will need to be taken. Unfortunately, there are a host of couples whose idealism so completely overrides their realism about marriage that they enter this blessed estate blind to possible problems. When they hear the statement 'the honeymoon is over', they take it as just another joke about marriage. They fail to realise that adjustments inevitably need to be made which did not surface in courtship and the relatively short 'honeymoon euphoria' after marriage.

For practical purposes this chapter is designed to point out the kinds of conditions that place marriages in jeopardy. These conditions are reasonably predictable. They are based upon the developmental or growth stages of the individuals involved, the types of environmental pressures they face, and the unique nature of the conflicts in the marriage relationship itself. The special risks of the early and middle years of marriage are the major topics presented.

Early years

There are differences of opinion as to what constitutes the 'early years' as compared to the 'mid-life' crisis. The early years will be considered largely as the twenties and early thirties, while the mid-life will encompass the period beginning in the mid-thirties, and continuing through the forties.

Developmental stages differ depending upon the length of the marriage, the characteristics of those involved, unique experiences the couples have gone through and many other factors. This treatise, however, is directed largely to typical marital relation-ships. The danger of stereotyping people is always present when time periods are delineated but there is general agreement that likely risks can be fairly well documented through research, pro-fessional counsellors, marriage clinics and the individuals them-selves.

The risk of being uncommitted

One young man is known to have said to the girl he wanted to marry: 'I want you to understand that divorce will always be an option for us if we become unhappy living together.' He saw marriage as a contract with an 'escape clause'. Such is the pre-vailing attitude of many as they enter the early years of their marriage. Convenience, comfort, and security in the relationship takes precedence over loyalty and commitment to each other 'until ,death us do part'.

Bill Borden, an outstanding missionary, summed up his dedi-cation to the ministry. He said, 'No reserve, no retreat, no regret!' We need this kind of commitment in sacred marriage relationships as well.

Psychologically, commitment involves the total person: intellect, feeling and will. In the final analysis, however, the will determines the seriousness of commitment. Feelings may change depending upon circumstances. Love may be masked by resentments and leave husbands and wives insensitive and confused about true feelings for each other. Intellectually, one may fail to form accurate con-clusions due to lack of information or the tendency to rationalise. The will, however, is like the 'north star' in the universe that maintains a point of reference. Commitment is the adhesive which holds people together through such everyday problems as balancing the budget, working through sexual incompatibility, or adjusting to in-laws. Vacillation in commitment is hazardous, and allows marriages to fall apart. The uncommitted are unhappy and unful-filled, and their marriages often ultimately fail.

The risk of bitterness

Most people know how to handle their 'love life' better than they do their 'hate life'. In the broad spectrum of problems that are faced by marriage counsellors it becomes evident that one of the most frequent is the problem of bitterness or resentment. The love-hate conflicts in early marriage develop in many areas. If marriage partners would face and resolve their angers, the tranquillity of their marriage would be considerably enhanced. Unfortunately, however, many people repress or hold down their anger for long periods of time and make no attempt to share and 'work through' how they really feel. Anger thus develops into deep-seated resentments or bitterness.

Inability to deal with bitterness is one of the main reasons why wives or husbands begin to question their real love for each other. It is like having a balancing set of scales and each time an 'ounce' of love is placed on one side, an 'ounce' of hate is placed on the other. Hate tends to negate the feeling and expression of love and leaves the individual emotionally flat or apathetic. Often a wife or husband starts to feel that perhaps they have 'fallen out' of love. When partners begin to question their love for each other the marriage relationship loses one of its main motivations for existence and begins to deteriorate.

The reader may ask, 'But how do you handle resentment and allow love to come through?' Although sharing and understanding are important, the ultimate answer is forgiveness. Perhaps more marriages are destroyed through lack of forgiveness than any other factor. If a person cannot forgive, he cannot truly love. Forgiveness, as demonstrated by our Lord, is one of the greatest expressions of love. When a wife or husband forgives, and is forgiven by God, resentments disappear and they rediscover their love for each other.

The next question that may be asked is, 'Why don't husbands and wives forgive more than they do?' Much could be written at this point, but the following reasons cover most of the problems.

One of the major barriers is pride, or the unwillingness to humble oneself. Some people don't forgive because they think forgiveness is agreement. To some, forgiveness is weakness, and to others they think the other person does not deserve forgiveness because of the terrible things they have done. Self-righteous people will not forgive. Others place conditions upon their forgiveness, saying 'If you will do this, then I will forgive you'. Jesus placed no specific human conditions on forgiveness but said, 'Father, forgive them; for they know not what they do' (Luke 23:34). Finally, there are those who want the other person to suffer awhile before they forgive them, and some want revenge first.

The risk of not leaving parents

'To leave or not to leave, that is the question.' Not long ago a young wife moved some distance from her parents. One day she dogmatically announced, 'I'm going to call my parents every week whether my husband likes it or not!' Her consideration to call her parents was commendable, but her attitude was uncompromising and insensitive as it related to her husband. Of all the risks in marriage it is generally agreed that the three main ones are money, sex, and in-laws, but not necessarily in this order.

When God's word refers to the institution of marriage it says: 'From the beginning of the creation God made them male and female. For this cause shall a man leave his father and mother, and cleave to his wife. . . . What therefore God hath joined together, let not man put asunder' (Mark 10:6, 7, 9). God anticipated the risks involved relative to the time when children get married and leave home. Many parents, and children as well, have difficulty with the word 'leave' because they interpret it to mean to abandon. To abandon means literally to forsake or desert, and this concept is neither scriptural nor humane. To cleave, on the other hand, means to adhere, cling, and be faithful to one's mate in such a manner that there is never a question as to whose 'flesh' a married partner belongs to in this world. The Bible teaches that the union of husband and wife in marriage should be so complete that the two are 'one flesh' (Mark 10:8). The fusion of 'flesh' in marriage transcends any other attachment in life, and is superseded only by one's union with God in spirit (Luke 14:26).

Failure to understand and accept what it means to leave parents and cleave to one's spouse places many marriages, especially in the early years, in the high risk category. Part of the problem develops because husbands and wives, although they have left their parents physically, cannot emotionally leave them and put their mate first. For various reasons their emotional attachments have been so fixed on one or both of their parents that they find difficulty in redirecting their love sufficiently toward their mate. Often this is related to excessive dependence carried over from childhood.

Because parents have so much to do with the development of conscience, their children are sometimes made to feel unusually guilty about separation. The wife or husband is caught between unnecessary guilt created by the parents and love for their spouse. In this kind of dilemma some married men and women repudiate their parents altogether, while others cling excessively to them and thus alienate their mate. This produces conflicts and feelings that place their marriage in serious jeopardy.

In the final analysis, even though parents may perpetuate excessive attachments and immature patterns of behaviour, the decision to leave and cleave is the responsibility of the husband or wife before God. The risk is too high to do otherwise.

The risk of misunderstanding your mate

Understanding the opposite sex has been the brunt of many jokes, especially relative to understanding women. In the early years of marriage, however, the smile often disappears when misunderstanding makes the difference between divorce and a successful marriage. Ignorance is not bliss when it comes to misunderstanding your mate!

Men and women are different in many ways and failure to understand this creates needless conflicts in marriage. The gender and physical characteristics of men and women are common knowledge, but often little is known about the psychological differences that are extremely important. For example, men and women differ in their emphasis upon thinking as compared to feeling. The average husband places more emphasis upon rational, factual and systematic thinking than his wife and is less aware of feelings and emotions. Women tend to be more 'personal' and show deeper interest in feelings. If a man, for example, is grilling steaks and you ask him where he purchased them he will promptly give you the name of the butcher's shop or store. On the other hand, if a woman is grilling steaks and you ask her where she bought them she is more likely to say, 'Why, what's the matter with them?'

Generally, men are do-ers, while women are be-ers. Men are achievement orientated and tend to be more aggressive than women. A woman usually is more interested in being and expressing herself than achieving. For this reason, women are more vulnerable, in general, to criticism. Their self-concept or self-image as a wife or mother is more quickly shattered than that of their husband. Men are ordinarily more self-confident and ego-orientated and do not react to criticism as seriously as women. A husband who continually criticises his wife runs the risk of destroying her self-esteem or self-respect. She is especially sensitive in the areas pertaining to her feminine role. She wants to be treated in a feminine manner and be given credit for her unique feminine contributions, although this has changed somewhat in the last decade. Although men are less sensitive to criticism than women they are especially affected by criticism directed toward their masculinity, challenging their male ego or image, and their capacity to earn a living. Some men react with physical violence to these sort of insults.

In the light of the above differences, it is possible for husbands and wives to anticipate many actions and reactions in their mates. Just as 'defensive driving' with an automobile reduces the risks on the highway, understanding the unique characteristics of the opposite sex can minimise unnecessary conflicts and frustrations.

The risk of immaturity

Frequently teenagers ask the question, 'How old should you be when you get married?' My initial answer is that chronological age is not the only age that should be considered. It is my practice to encourage them to ask themselves the question, 'How old am I emotionally, socially, morally, and spiritually?' There are a host of marriages where either, or both, husband and wife are mature in some areas of their development, but very immature in others. Immaturity places undue strains upon a marriage and increases the risk of breakdown or unhappiness.

Major areas of immaturity include the inability to make decisions because of excessive dependence, lack of emotional controls to the extent that a marriage partner has 'temper tantrums' or cries excessively, exaggerated self-pity which develops into a 'martyr complex', and the habit of over-reacting emotionally to little things and 'making mountains out of mole hills'.

Due to the high risk of letting immaturity destroy a marriage or adversely affect the children, husbands and wives need to examine their respective roles in this regard. The advice 'Act your age!' is appropriate at all ages. Unfortunately, when adults act like children it is tempting for others to treat them like children, and this is damaging to the development of a mature marriage relationship.

Mid-life

The risk of an identity crisis

'I'm trying to find myself' is a standard answer given today by people who are on the verge of divorce after having been married 15 years or more. When a counsellor asks them how they would answer the questions, 'Who am I?' and 'Where am I going?' they do not know the answers. Usually the term 'identity crisis' has been reserved for teenagers who were trying to find their way in the 'no man's land' between childhood and adulthood. In today's world this term now applies also to those adults who are lost on a trackless journey through mid-life without the compass of experience or information to guide them.

It is a time to expose the myth that adults are fully developed, static, unchanging and, therefore, extremely boring subjects to study. Quite the contrary: for many, mid-life today is a time of disillusionment, reassessment and incompleteness. It becomes a time of 'burn-out' or being 'born again' for some. Married couples at this age are caught between the generations of their adolescent children and ageing parents, between the decision either to recommit themselves to their marriage or to have an 'affair'. Yes, it is the time when mum and dad are forced to answer the questions, 'Who am I?' and 'Where am I going?'

The risks of an identity crisis: men

'What happens to a man in mid-life when he reaches the top of the mountain in his career and he sees no more mountains to climb? Is the rest of his life a plateau?' These are the questions of many men in mid-life today. The challenge has gone out of life and they feel a sense of staleness and boredom. 'What happens to a man in mid-life when it dawns upon him that he will never reach the top of the mountain in his career? Is he doomed to fail the rest of his life?' Many men think these thoughts and feel a sense of helplessness and failure.

Fortunately, there are answers to these questions if a man will honestly reassess his life and work. Unfortunately, however, too many men react to this mid-life crisis by impulsively attempting a radical change in their life-style. They have already asked themselves, 'Is this all there is to life after all this work?' and they begin to experiment blindly with a new life-style outside their family, their morals and God. Rather than taking the identity crisis as a challenge in mid-life they seek to escape in various self-defeating ways.

The toughest challenges to face are not necessarily concerned with work, but with love and marriage. In the first place, when a man's identity or unity and understanding of himself wavers it affects his ability to enjoy intimacy. Relationships, often with his wife and children, which have been rich and rewarding in the past become dull and boring. This causes him to question his love for those closest to him, especially his wife. His problems tend to focus on his marriage and he frequently blames his marriage for his condition. Granted that there are some marriages that need a 'tune-up' or even an 'overhaul', a shaky marriage is usually not the cause of his mid-life crisis, but rather the result.

It is not surprising that in mid-life one-fourth of all marriages of 15 years or more end in divorce. In the years between 1976 and 1981 in the USA divorce among couples married 20 years or more doubled. Often, finding a new partner temporarily appears to be a simple solution to cover up the complex problems involved in making a marriage work. Many men who fall short of divorce become involved in sexual infidelity. These diversions become an escape from creative solutions and the courage to honour sacred commitments. Their 'novelty' appears to be a 'quick-fix' to counteract boredom.

Of course, not all retreats among men into divorce and 'affairs' can be attributed to sexual motivation. In the mid-life crisis the ego needs are more responsible for infidelity than sexual ones. Clandestine sex brings some sense of 'accomplishment'. Then, too, since adults are youth-orientated and the ageing process has set in, men are also 'proving' themselves insofar as virility and manliness are concerned in extra-marital sexual exploits.

You, as a reader, may say at this stage, 'So much for the description and explanation of the mid-life crisis, but how about the solution?' Please be assured that there are constructive, creative and challenging solutions. They start with an admission of a mid-life crisis, a sincere desire to change, and awareness of both the internal and external resources available.

Although external resources, such as professional counselling and better support from the family and church are important, keep in mind that internal resources are by far the most helpful in recovery. Inner spiritual growth is the greatest asset. Also, many men suffer from a 'collapse of causes' and need bigger and better things to live for than materialistic and career goals. Reassessment of an individual's whole value system relative to what is most important and worthwhile in life is needed. Rearrangement of priorities in the use of time spent with the wife and family should be high on the list of changes.

In this 'mid-course correction' explore possibilities for the rest of your life. Relative to career, decide whether you want to begin a new one or find ways to reassess and renew your present one. Don't underestimate the importance of such approaches as physical exercise, hobbies, attention to rest and eating, change of scenery from time to time and talking with your wife about pressures. Above all, pray and read God's word. Don't forget that God has a plan for the rest of your life!

The risks of an identity crisis: women

The lyrics of a recent popular song, 'The Friday Night Blues', depicted the dilemma of mid-life in which the husband came home tired and exhausted from a busy week at the job and was taking off his shoes to relax and stay at home. On the other hand, his wife had been home all week with her work and the children, and was putting on her shoes to go out and have a good time doing something different. They both had the Friday night blues, but for different reasons!

The average wife and husband at mid-life tend to reverse their interests and life-style in the crisis of wanting something more out of life. As mentioned earlier, in the early years the husbands are the do-ers who are captivated by their career and drive for achievement, while the wives are the be-ers who strive to be good wives and mothers with the emphasis upon feeling and person-centred living. In the crisis of change at mid-life it is the husband who is tired of doing and needs to be more person and feeling-centred, while his wife feels the need, since her mother-role is almost over, to begin doing different things outside the home.

In mid-life men may sense a limitation of time, slow down on career development, become more interested in their emotional and introspective side, desire to be more home orientated, sense a diminishing or uncertain sex drive, and have a mood of despair come over them. Women, quite to the contrary, may experience a feeling of an expansion of time, become more excited about a career, discover their competitive and assertive side, want to be home less, have a greater sexual awareness and their mood is more of hope than despair.

At mid-life women need more social contact outside the home and sometimes feel, along with their husband, that they have made an over-investment in the role of a parent. Wives begin to question whether it has been wise to draw all their emotional sustenance from their husbands and feel they need more friends. Many of them feel that their husband has been a good man but not good enough and the idealism of the early years of marriage has been replaced by the realism of the mid-life crisis. Some wives begin to pity themselves, resent their husband and family, and rebellion often takes place in the less mature and stable women.

Frequently this rebellion and search for a less constricted life is expressed either in an affair or in divorce. The average mother sends her child off to school when she is 35 and she re-enters the working world. Other women, already divorced, take new husbands. They become more adventurous in their reaction to boredom and get a panic feeling that time is running out for them.

At this stage in a mid-life crisis, just as with her husband, there must be an honest admission of a crisis, a sincere desire to change, and an awareness of available resources. It is a time when commitments need to be deepened, and it is a time for self-confrontation. Sooner or later, depending upon how open the communication channels are with her husband, there needs to be a reconciliation and an open sharing of hurt feelings and different points of view.

Fortunately, as a general rule, a woman is more open to seeking a professional marriage counsellor than her counterpart and tends to come to counselling first. They have fewer inhibitions in talking about their problems and exploring possibilities of what they want to become for the rest of their lives.

Hopefully, of course, it will be possible for her husband to participate in the whole counselling process. Resistance from the husband, such as, 'I am not crazy', 'My wife needs help, not me', and 'There are worse marriages than ours', needs to be overcome. Sometimes the encouragement of someone else in the family, a good friend or a minister, will help. It is important, however, that they seek a competent Christian counsellor whom they can trust, who shares their religious values. If possible, attending a marriage enrichment seminar is suggested. Also, there are good books about the mid-life crisis that can be helpful.

The risk of missing God's will

Consider the statement, 'The will of God, nothing more, nothing less, nothing else!' This emphasis upon God's will for everyone, including wives and husbands, is biblically sound (Matthew 7:21-23). In describing, explaining and offering suggestions about how to deal with the risks in marriage it would be a gross mistake for me not to include the risk of missing God's will in marriage. God has an 'ideal' will for every life and many fall short of it. He also has a 'circumstantial' will in which he deals with people in the stream of circumstances created by ignorance, tragedy and sin, and weaves a new life within his will. In addition, he has a 'permissive' will in which he allows things to happen that shape and discipline his children like nothing else ever could. Search the Scriptures, seek the advice of good people, and pray earnestly for divine revelation in discovering what it takes to enrich your marriage or repair damaged feelings and commitments. It is quite possible that your mate may never change completely, but God's word says, 'My grace is sufficient for thee: for my strength is made perfect in weakness' (2 Corinthians 12:9).

Many have sincerely prayed, 'Lord change me', and have seen their marriage revitalised and revolutionised to the glory of God. For every risk, God has a remedy—ask him!

Part Three
We are a family

'WE have three children. Their names are as follows: Felix, aged 12; Pareshkumar, aged 11; Sukirtiben, aged eight. We are in Bombay. Our children are in boarding school at Anand, 400 kilometres away. We are glad for them to be studying in a Christian atmosphere.'

William Keshav (India)

'Holy Father, in Thy mercy
Hear our anxious prayer;
Keep our loved ones, now far distant,
'Neath Thy care.'

Isabella S. Stevenson

'Cornelia kept her in talk till her children came from school, and these, said she, are my jewels.'
From the works of Robert Burton (1577-1640)

'In the dedication of this child you desire to give him fully to God and you want him to love God and only and always do his will. You are willing that he shall spend all his life for God and give himself to the service of Jesus Christ. As far as you can you must keep from him all intoxicating drink, tobacco, harmful reading, and every other influence which may injure him in mind or body. You must teach and train him to be a faithful servant of Jesus Christ.'
From Salvation Army Ceremonies
(Dedication of children)

9

Togetherness during the hard times
Captain and Mrs Ted and Dianne Palmer (Canada)

IT doesn't matter where you build your home; the storms of life will eventually strike it. At that time, it will matter very much on what you have built. 'Therefore whosoever heareth these sayings of mine, and doeth them, I will liken him unto a wise man, which built his house upon a rock: And the rain descended, and the floods came, and the winds blew, and beat upon that house; and it fell not: for it was founded upon a rock' (Matthew 7:24, 25).

Christian homes are not immune from the major crises of life. Indeed, God often uses the times of greatest family difficulty to manifest his reality in an unforgettable way.

Storms test our foundations. The degree of steadiness our marriages and homes manifest in the worst of times will be the degree of our witness to other homes around us.

Illness

Because holy living and Christ's forgiveness free them from the debilitating tensions of guilt, Christians do have an 'edge' in the direction of good health, but this does not guarantee that serious illness will not occur.

We live in a fallen world, a world that groans under Satan's influence. In a sense, therefore, all sickness is a result of sin in the world. However, family members must never add the weight of guilt to the burden of illness. Any talking or even thinking about 'What sin is God punishing you for?' is unproductive, unhealthy and wrong. Satan uses sickness to destroy our relationships with each other and with God. Our heavenly Father uses illness as a means to strengthen those same relationships.

Sickness can glorify God as well as mature our relationships. This biblical principle is manifested clearly in Christ's healing of the man blind from birth (John 9). Family members should be open to the spiritual procedures outlined in James 5:14, 15. The father and mother can act as the elders of the little congregation that constitutes a home. Or the leaders of the corps can be called to fulfil these directions. All this must be done, however, with the motive of glorifying God, not just as an escape from inconvenience, discomfort, or pain.

Family members must assist each other during long, chronic, or terminal illness by sharing reminders that God glorifies himself through his sustaining power as well as through his healing power. Some of God's most effective witnesses are those in whom his grace is apparent as they are confined to a hospital bed or wheelchair. Paul's chronic condition, his 'thorn in the flesh' (2 Corinthians 12:7), was used in just such a way. Dads and mums, husbands and wives, brothers and sisters, sons and daughters must help the sick person to live one day at a time, believing that God has a purpose to fulfil in their life on that particular day.

An awareness of potential spiritual dangers will be helpful if we are to avoid falling into spiritual ill health during a time of physical sickness. Pain is a very personal and compelling experience. The sick person's natural human tendency toward self-centredness can, therefore, be felt and amplified by his physical ordeal. The question, 'Why me?' can become obsessive.

In addition, the sick person can gradually become more and more resentful of family members who are healthy. The question becomes, 'Why not him (or her)?' This bitterness not only makes the person less responsive to the ministrations of his family, but also blocks the healing and sustaining work of the Holy Spirit.

Ultimately, the one who is coping with illness can imitate Job's spiritual descent (Job 3:1-3) and question God's right or God's motive for organising his life as he is doing. By such an attitude the person becomes a rebel against the very one who could help him most. He, therefore, deteriorates rather than benefits from the trial God has allowed to come his way.

Illness can and must be viewed as a spiritual opportunity. Paul saw his physical problem as a means whereby he could experience a larger portion of God's grace than had ever been his before: 'Therefore I take pleasure in infirmities, in reproaches, in necessities, in persecutions, in distresses for Christ's sake: for when I am weak, then am I strong' (2 Corinthians 12:10). Our spouse or other family member must be encouraged to be prayerful and trusting (rather than non-communicative and rebellious) during illness. To realise one's desperate need for God's help is the first step in receiving that help or grace. God often uses dark physical experiences to frame and highlight his bright, beautiful working in the spirit of a person.

Illness can also provide the aggressive and confident person with one of his or her first experiences in receiving love. Unable to run the show and make himself necessary in the lives of others, he experiences what it means for them to be necessary to him. As he depends on the practical help, encouragement and prayers of his spouse and other family members, he will experience love in a remarkable and memorable way. The hand that brings the cold cloth for his forehead and feeds him at meal-times is saying, 'I love you'. The lips that read him a newspaper article, a devotional booklet, or a Scripture portion are saying 'I love you' with each word that is read. Sponge baths, a flower on the dinner tray, fresh bed clothes, the provision of his favourite music (perhaps on tape) and the uncomplaining, and seemingly unending, clean-up jobs are beautiful manifestations of love. Many people have found that their worst times physically have turned out to be their best times as far as quality and quantity of love are concerned.

Family members who are experiencing chronic physical weakness or convalescing from major surgery must be helped to see that God has a purpose for those days of confinement. Jesus told his disciples to 'Come ye yourselves apart . . . and rest a while' (Mark 6:31). Many of us are so activity orientated that we have never obeyed that instruction. Illness may provide an opportunity to do so.

During these days, therefore, definite spiritual projects could be established. These might involve:

1 a re-reading of all or part of the Bible;
2 writing letters of witness to unsaved friends and relatives;
3 studying some good Christian books;
4 times of intensive prayer.

A husband or wife, a father or mother, can keep the invalid accountable for the progress of such a project. A simple 'How are you coming with that book?' or 'What did God teach you through your Bible reading today?' will help the patient to keep working at his project.

The pain and frustration of ill health are inescapable realities. However, members of a Christian family can help their sick loved one to get maximum spiritual value out of this common human experience.

Bereavement

Both family and faith in Christ mean most when death pays a visit. Human beings seem both unwilling and unable to simply wander off and die by themselves as do old elephants. But, no matter how many or magnificent are the human beings holding one's hand, death would still be an experience in despair were not Christ's hand reaching out as well.

There are two types of visits death pays to a home. In the one instance, he sends his calling card and the family knows for weeks or months that their loved one will be taken. On the other hand, death often pays a surprise visit in an industrial or automobile accident; sometimes a sudden, fatal heart attack or brain failure takes someone who appears to be in the prime of life and the best of health.

However, a Christian is ready spiritually and ought to be ready emotionally and mentally at any time. The Bible reminds us that 'ye know not what shall be on the morrow. For what is your life? It is even a vapour, that appeareth for a little time, and then vanisheth away' (James 4:14). Mates and parents have a responsibility to develop a state of readiness within the family circle so that the visit does not come as a completely unforeseen and irrational imposition.

Husbands and wives should take time to share with each other and ask, 'What would you do if I were to die tomorrow?'. Response to this question should cover many facets of reality: funeral arrangements, insurance policies, mortgage payments, employment possibilities, child rearing, sources of emotional support, understanding of death in its spiritual context. Similarly, though death should not be a preoccupation in family discussions, it should be dealt with as opportunities arise during family devotions and sharing times. Children will inherit a fearfulness about death if the parents demonstrate by word or action that they themselves cannot face it squarely.

What spiritual principle underlies a healthy attitude toward death? It is the principle of God's proprietorship.

We must understand, appreciate and accept the fact that God created us; we belong to him. He does, however, give us 'on loan' others of his children to share in our lives. We must thank him for our mate and our children and for each day that we experience life together. But we must never forget that they belong to him. They are subject to recall at any time. 'There is no man that hath power over the spirit to retain the spirit; neither hath he power in the day of death' (Ecclesiastes 8:8).

God's word reminds us that 'whether we live, we live unto the Lord; and whether we die, we die unto the Lord: whether we live therefore, or die, we are the Lord's' (Romans 14:8).

The death of a loved one never comes at the right time as far as we are concerned. The deceased is too young, or is still needed too much; he is just a few months from a 60th anniversary or just finishing a degree at college. We have a hundred reasons for arguing that he should have been given another month, another decade, or a further half-century of living.

Death's visit to the home is, therefore, one of the ultimate tests of faith. Do we trust God? Do we really believe that he knows what he is doing? Are we convinced that his sense of timing is better than ours? Can we say in the midst of the emotional ordeal of separation that 'we know that *all things* work together for good to them that love God, to them who are the called according to his purpose' (Romans 8:28)?

Such trust must be learned and taught day by day within the family circle so that even during bereavement our marriage and family can glorify God and speak a message of hope to others.

When a spouse or child dies, there are certain spiritual dangers to prepare for and surmount:

1 Avoid self-reproach. The 'why didn't I do more for him (her)?' attitude achieves nothing. Our sins of omission can be confessed to God and total forgiveness experienced. If Jesus is never going to 'bring them up against me any more', why should we chain ourselves with them?

2 Avoid self-pity. 'Why did this happen to me?' implies that it ought better to have happened to others. Such thinking betrays an infantile self-centredness. Confess this sin, claim the promise of Romans 8:28, and seek to discover what God wants you to learn and how he wants you to grow through this tough experience.

3 Plan a productive future. No event, no matter how traumatic, should be allowed to control the rest of your life. God has given you additional days, months, or years of life so that you can fulfil his will in you, for you and through you. Had Catherine Marshall allowed herself the expense of bitterness and resentment after her husband's early death, the world would never have benefited from her ministry through the written word.

4 Do not be afraid to give expression to your grief. Inhibiting your sorrow might easily result in emotional or psychological difficulties which a normal or healthy expression of sorrow would avoid.

Some people, suffering the loss of a loved one, lose themselves in an alcoholic or drug-induced stupor. Some fling themselves into a new marriage or pregnancy. Others will use the grieving process as an excuse for attention-getting or immorality.

No radical decision-making should occur in the midst of the grief period. The bereaved person needs lots of time to work through and to talk through his or her feelings, particularly as they relate to fears of and hopes for the future.

This is where the ministry of the family is crucial. When a mother, father, or child dies the remaining members of the family must, subsequent to the busy crowded days of the public mourning and funeral, be prepared to take plenty of time with each other so that emotional wounds are thoroughly healed and not just permanently camouflaged, festering forever under a band-aid of superficial normality.

Family Bible study, prayer, sharing times and fun are essential for this ministry of healing to take place. Both the love of each for the other and the love of God for the family can become more real as the experience of loss is dealt with on the basis of his proprietorship and with the help of his comforting power.

Unemployment

Job loss is one of the most shattering experiences of life. It devastates a person's self-image. Also, by reducing income radically, it amplifies economic pressures to such a level that they become the family's major preoccupation. Marriages break down; children insult their parents; fathers and mothers frequently lose control in dealing with their sons and daughters.

The first thing to remember is that God intends you to work: 'For even when we were with you, this we commanded you, that if any would not work, neither should he eat' (2 Thessalonians 3:10). Our appropriate purpose is labour, not leisure (Genesis 3:19). Therefore, fervent prayer that God will provide employment is well within the will of God. His affirmative response can be expected.

Often, however, considerable time can lapse between the beginning of such prayer and God's delivering of a job. This period of delay can be a terrible time of doubting and tension (in which case the spirituality of all members of the family will suffer) or it can be a tremendous time of trusting and peace. If the latter is true, the family will grow together spiritually during the period of joblessness.

Husband and wife should carefully review the family finances as soon as the lay-off or firing occurs. Once they have gathered the facts concerning their income and expenses, they should arrive at an austerity budget reflecting the change in cash-flow level.

Then, if there are children, approximately eight years of age or older, the offspring should be informed, in a family sharing time, of the change in finances. The actual budget can be explained, particularly pointing out those points at which their personal desires will be affected. There can be time for questions. The purpose of this briefing is to enlist the co-operation of the family members in keeping expenses within the new budget levels. Efforts to maintain the former lifestyle is a costly sham; failure to give youngsters information to help them understand will result in conflict as they confront seemingly arbitrary changes with rebelliousness and antagonism.

This sharing time should end with a short 'testimony' from the breadwinner in which he explains that he is totally without any means of livelihood and that he has no prospects in view. He can then proceed to explain that, having reached the end of his resources, he is prepared to trust God to provide the job that the family needs. This 'family council' should end with a time of open prayer.

The breadwinner has announced that he is going to trust God for a means to provide his 'daily bread'. Now he must live a life of trust before his family so that their level of faith will be encouraged.

To manifest trust, he must avoid worry. Matthew 6:25-33 will be the basis of his 'one day at a time' faith that God will provide the food, drink and clothing that he and his family need.

In addition, the quantity and intensity of his praying will increase. Freed from the confines of regular working hours, he can afford more time to pray. Indeed, he cannot afford not to pray! Matthew 7:7-11 will assure him that our heavenly Father is both a listening and a loving God. And, knowing the promise that 'if we ask any thing according to his will, he heareth us' (1 John 5:14), he will be confident that God's answer is only a time away.

Prayerful trust in God does not exclude, but rather necessitates, energetic and imaginative job hunting. Because God is on your side does not mean that you don't need to work at job hunting as hard as would a non-Christian. 'Stepping out in faith' is not done from a reclining chair in one's living room. Be open to an entirely new type of employment opportunity. God may be moving you into an extremely different job environment or career direction. Don't reject his will by clinging to your usual 'trade', your previous 'status' or your prior level of remuneration. Either for your own sake or for that of those to whom he is sending you to witness, he may have something for you that lies quite outside your normal expectations.

There are, therefore, both spiritual dangers (discouragement, loss of faith) and spiritual opportunities (closeness to God, excitement of the anticipated miracle) in joblessness. However, there are physical and mental dangers as well. Through sleeping in, sitting around, watching TV and reading, one can gradually lose the habit of working. God soundly condemns all sluggishness (Proverbs 6:6-11). It is, therefore, important for the jobless person to stick as close as possible to a working man's timetable for rising and retiring. And it is essential that he plan productive activities to fill his time, whether these be home repairs (ones that consume time rather than money!) or volunteer work with a local charity or the Army.

Keep God in the centre of your focus. A job is simply a means to an end (food on the table). God himself is the end for which we live. Remember his command and promise: 'Seek ye first the kingdom of God, and his righteousness; and all these things shall be added unto you' (Matthew 6:33).

Pulling up stakes

Although millions of people have survived—indeed thrived!—subsequent to migration experiences that took them half-way around the world, we must never presume that a family move is always an easy or beneficial event.

Too often, men have expected enthusiasm over a relocation of their family when no one but the father had anything to gain from the change. In order to 'sell' his mate and children on a move which he has accepted to advance his career, dad will often entice positive response by announcing his salary and encouraging the children to imagine all the material benefits that will be theirs.

Such an approach, especially in a Christian context, is reprehensible. As parents, we want our children to grow up learning to seek and follow God's will, not simply to pursue their own material advantages. Years of Sunday-school training and Bible messages can be undone when so significant a question as 'Where are we going to live?' is decided primarily on the basis of how much worldly wealth will be ours if we live there.

Before a final decision is made about moving a family, the father should carefully discuss all the implications of the move with his wife and the couple should subsequently share their concerns and vision with their children.

According to the Bible, God is the governor of the movements of those families that belong to him: 'Now the Lord had said unto Abram, "Get thee out of thy country, and from thy kindred, and from thy father's house, unto a land that I will show thee"' (Genesis 12:1). In Hebrews 11:8-11 Abraham's response to God's leading is explained as a manifestation of faith. He went where God wanted him to go, following an inner leading rather than simply responding to an external enticement.

The decision-making process that precedes a family move will give your family an excellent opportunity to be sensitive to each other and to the will of God. Each family member should be encouraged to show his or her feelings about the proposed move. This sharing should be done in a non-judgmental, non-argumentative environment. Because a family move ranks among the most important decisions that ever faces a home, the process itself can be a valuable learning experience. If the family as a group and its members as individuals can learn something about godly decision making, then they have acquired a life skill of inestimable value.

Read Acts 15:1-34 and observe a Christian community in the midst of a decision-making process. Note the stages in this process:

1 Getting together (verses 2, 4, 6);
2 Getting the facts (verses 7-11, 12);
3 Getting the word (verses 15-17, 21);
4 Getting an interpretation, eg from elder or parent (verses 13, 15, 19, 20);
5 Getting at it! (verses 22-31).

Ultimately, it is the father, in consultation with his wife, who will make the actual decision. But he is truly a wise father who listens carefully to the facts his family shares, including the fact of how they feel about the relocation being considered. And he is truly a son of his heavenly Father who also listens to God's word and to the quiet voice of the Holy Spirit.

Before he reaches his informed decision, the father may feel the need to provide the family and himself with time for further prayer. He must know that he is within the will of God in saying 'Yes!' to the move. If not, he will find himself and his family subject to numerous complications, frustrations and spiritual dangers.

Should God's direction lead to a decision to 'pull up stakes', the family breadwinner must be aware that packing up the household effects is only the beginning of his responsibilities. One of the biggest and most essential duties of the father is to make sure that his wife and children are guided and assisted through the period of re-adjustment to the new community. Too often the father throws himself so totally into impressing his superiors in his new position that he takes no time to pastor his wife and children during an anxious time in their lives. The family will be surrounded by a new house or apartment, by new stores and schools, by new sports teams, clubs and a new congregation. In the midst of all that flux and instability should be a determined emphasis on that which has not changed—the little community we call a family.

There should be extra family nights—times for recreation, sharing and prayer. Dad and mum should make sure they go out *together* in the new community so that from the first people will see them as a couple. Dad should help in resolving some of the complications: for example, registering the children in school, learning about bus routes, locating stores where school supplies and other personal needs can be obtained, discovering where parks, arenas and other recreational facilities are located.

With a deep trust in God and a firm sense of family support, a period of relocation can be an experience of growth. To attempt it on any other basis is to try to move an ocean liner out of port with a mutinous crew and no pilot aboard!

The emptying nest

In her study of the major *Passages* of life, Gail Sheehy writes that a most poignant aspect of the middle years concerns the children who are slipping away. Sociologist Virginia Satir lists 10 predictable crises that a family undergoes: 'The fifth is when the child has grown to adulthood and is leaving home to seek his independence. There are often heavy loss feelings here.'

Unfortunately, parental fearfulness about this inevitable experience of loss often results in a repression of all thoughts about it. They no more wish to contemplate the loss of their children through leaving home than they would want to meditate on the loss of each other through death. Yet God has given parents a definite responsibility of not only facing the fact of parting, but preparing their offspring for it.

The preparation for this difficult experience must begin as soon as a child is born. Christians should never treat others as a means of meeting their own needs. This includes our children. Some parents have such a need to be needed that they early develop a dependency on their children far beyond that which the children have on them. They have used the children to meet their own needs rather than investing their own lives in meeting the real, long-term needs of their children.

Secondly, husbands and wives must always avoid the trap of relating to each other primarily or totally through the children. If you fall into this trap, you will indeed be unwilling to let your children depart for you realise that you and your mate have no relationship without them.

Children are a temporary part of a home. God never intended us to build our homes around the children. Our responsibility is rather to prepare them to build their own homes, especially to build them around God. 'Therefore shall a man leave his father and his mother . . .' (Genesis 2:24). Isaac calls his son Jacob to him and tells him to

'Arise, go to Padanaram, to the house of Bethuel thy mother's father; and take thee a wife from thence' (Genesis 28:2).

Christian parents should not be postponing departure, but preparing their sons and daughters for it. In fact, the granting of additional privileges and the corresponding imposition of responsibilities during the adolescent years should always be seen as a preparation for independence. By the time your child is 18 he or she should be equipped by attitude and by skills to look after himself or herself. The maturing person should be taking pride in increasing levels of responsibility rather than boasting of his irresponsibility. Parents should gradually teach the basic practical living skills: money management (including taxes and insurance), cooking, sewing, household and car repairs, gardening and shopping.

When this positive, supportive and creative approach is taken, the child's departure will indeed be seen more as a graduation, rather than as a funeral.

Do you want a hope-filled family?

Christianity pivots on a few essential paradoxes. One of these is that the positive experiences we desire are attainable only through negative experiences we try to avoid. Jesus must die in order to confer eternal life upon us; our strength and self-confidence must decrease if the Holy Spirit is to grow strong within us; hope blossoms out of the tribulations that we fear.

Read Romans 5:1-4. Note that this principle works for believers only. The process starts with faith; the product is hope; the raw material is tribulation:

1 being justified by faith (verse 1)
2 we glory in tribulation (verse 3)
3 tribulation worketh patience (verse 3)
4 patience worketh experience (verse 4)
5 experience worketh hope (verse 4).

A Christian family is a very special team with at least two important purposes:

1 to glorify God
2 to grow toward spiritual maturity.

The hard times of life are essential in the achievement of both these purposes. Just as a soccer team never achieves greatness without clashing with difficult opponents, so we will never be all we want to be and all God wants us to be without facing, in a direct and faithful way, the painful challenges and crises that constitute the semi-finals on the way to life's 'World Cup'!

10

Bringing up children

Major and Mrs Joseph and Mary Larbi (Ghana)
Mrs Margaret Mead (South Africa)
(Our first contribution on this subject comes from Major and Mrs Larbi
of Ghana.—*Eds.*)

CHILDREN are a gift of God, to be loved, cared for and trained
for him. By our love towards our children we are to show them
what God's love is like. They must therefore be taught by example
and precept how to know and serve God. The school cannot replace
the Christian home and cannot give to children all the initial
training and guidance they need—guidance by which the
foundation for character is laid. It is important that parents should
know that the kind of persons their children will become in future is
largely determined by how they are brought up in the first five years
of their life. In a Christian family, therefore, the couple must be
particularly careful in guiding their children and caring for them
during this formative period, when their characters can be
moulded. However, even after that age, training and guidance are
important and should not be left to the school alone.

A Christian home should provide love, security and freedom, if
the personality of the child is to develop as God intends. Here are
some points which experience has taught us:

1 Discipline: Obedience should be expected from the child but
whenever possible reasons should be given for what we require a
child to do. Parents should be consistent and united in the demands
made and a child should not get from one parent what is denied
him by the other.

2 Encouragement: Say 'Well done' and encourage your child
when he deserves it or seems to need it. Be prepared to render an
apology to your child when you offend him or her unintentionally.

3 Confidence: Let the child feel that you are his support.

4 Questions: Children's questions must be answered patiently
and truthfully. If you don't know the answer, then say so. There is

no shame in this and you are training the child to be truthful. We are students all our lives.

5 Punishments: These should not be administered in fury. Tell the child *why* he is being punished.

6 Values: From the very beginning, parents must give their children training in cleanliness and pleasure in simplicity (for example, in clothing and footwear).

7 Routines: Parents will do a lot to safeguard their children's health by paying particular attention to the times of meals, going to bed, playing and exercise. Lastly, the devotional life of the parents should not be closed to their children. There should be habits of saying grace before and after meals and prayers at bedtime.

> How but in custom and in ceremony
> Are innocence and beauty born?
> *A Prayer for My Daughter,* William Butler Yeats

(More material about parents and children has been contributed by Mrs Margaret Mead of South Africa who has written the chapter on communication. Here is what she says about communicating with your children.—*Eds.*)

The more you communicate with your children, the less you will have to use punishment. Wisely-administered punishment is not cruel, but designed by God to teach the limits in a family. If discipline is consistent and loving, it is usually apparent fairly soon that the frequency of punishment becomes less and less. The children also feel much more secure when they know their limits and the consequences of overstepping them.

The wife has a duty to her husband and children to keep their father up to date on matters concerning the children. There are many men who feel cut off from their families for this very reason, and a better understanding all round can be achieved by communication in this area. It can happen that a man who is cut out of his family's day-to-day lives becomes very demanding and unreasonable in an attempt to get the attention he needs. Parents are partners in their responsibilities to their children.

There are a number of things we can do to ensure unity in our families:

1 Where both husband and wife are Christian believers, read the Bible both together with the family and privately, in order to learn God's way of doing things.

2 Praying aloud and together is most effective. Faith comes by hearing the word of God, and speaking the word brings light into all areas. The couple should pray for one another and thank God

for the various attributes of their partner. Involve the children in prayer. It will show them that God can be trusted. Share with them answers to prayer and so increase their faith.

3 If only one partner is a believer, avoid being self-righteous in your attitude. Allow God to work in your partner and your children in his own way, and present a loving attitude that will truly reflect God's power in your life.

4 Never use your children to manipulate your partner. And don't allow them to manipulate you either, especially one against the other. Be loyal to each other, particularly with regard to the handling of the children.

5 Do things together with your children. Make ordinary things special. Let your hair down sometimes and show them that you are human. A sense of humour is essential here. Use it often. But discourage the 'put down' type of humour which young people are very prone to use, as this is most destructive.

6 Don't be afraid to admit you're wrong. It is pointless to pretend perfection to your offspring. Sooner or later they will realise you are also human, and the later you leave it, the more traumatic the discovery.

7 Discipline in love, not anger. Discuss your children's problems with them, and encourage them to express themselves freely in this regard. This is invaluable for them in later life too. Don't react with shock or anger when they do share with you. This will discourage them from being honest with you on future occasions.

8 Never betray the private aspects of your discussions or confidences they share with you. If you do you will destroy their trust in you. Instead, try singing their praises from time to time, particularly when they are within earshot; but do it sincerely. This will have the effect of building up their self-image.

9 Love your wife or husband. There is no other one thing that you can do which will make your children feel more secure. Show your love for each other in their presence.

10 Endeavour to be consistent in discipline. This will require much help from above. The most natural thing to do is to allow misdemeanours of various intensities to pile up and then punish the child when you have reached 'the last straw' point. This is very confusing, especially to the small child, who won't be able to understand why he was punished for sniffing, for example, when outright disobedience such as breaking something valuable in a forbidden area or something equally serious was treated much more leniently. Parents need constantly to draw on the Lord for wisdom. There is nothing too small to bring to God in prayer.

11 Ask God to bridge the gap between the love this child needs and the love he or she receives, and then concentrate on his or her need for love.

12 Touch your children often. In this way you are expressing your love for them and teaching them to express tenderness in adulthood, an area where many adults have a problem.

13 Worship together. This essentially involves the husband and father in his role as spiritual head of the family. If he abdicates his responsibility, the wife should try gently to introduce the devotional aspect of family life. Many men (and some women too) are rather self-conscious about this, but helpful encouragement from their partner—sometimes over a period of years—can have the desired results. Children feel very secure when there is strong leadership from their parents with regard to worship, particularly when their father takes his spiritual responsibilities in the home seriously.

11

Let's talk about family prayer
Colonel and Mrs David and Alice Baxendale (USA)

DAVID: What about those things that make a Christian marriage? How do you build each other up in the faith? What about family praying and establishing the family altar? How do you teach the children by word and by example?

Alice: You'll forgive us if we fall back on our 30 years of living together, but these are the best examples, good and bad, that we know, so we want you to profit by our trial and error along with a host of those we know, friends we have observed, and scores we have counselled, prayed with, and with whom we have shared. What does the Bible say?

David: Joshua 4:6: 'That this may be a sign among you, that when your children ask their fathers in time to come, saying, What mean ye by these stones?'

Alice: Proverbs 22:6: 'Train up a child in the way he should go: and when he is old, he will not depart from it.'

David: Isaiah 54:13: 'And all thy children shall be taught of the Lord; and great shall be the peace of thy children.'

Alice:

> Prayer is the simplest form of speech
> That infant lips can try;
> Prayer the sublimest strains that reach
> The majesty on high.

David: These verses from the Bible and *The Song Book of The Salvation Army* would lead you to an easy conclusion on the question of the family altar and marriage. But you must work at it diligently to make it truly Christian. To be realistic, we must look at the fact, at the days in which we live, and be as honest but at the same time as spiritually optimistic as we can. We believe that a Christian marriage and a meaningful family altar can work on an everyday basis. To assert otherwise would be like kicking motherhood or down-grading apple-pie!

Alice: Now, we realise that for anyone with children, in a home where needs change with each birthday and demands upon your time change, it is a constant struggle to maintain a meaningful family altar. But we still believe it is possible if we work at it and build a strong spiritual life.

David: In every appointment we have received as Salvation Army officers, we could have found plausible excuses for not having family devotions. As corps officers, as staff members at the school for officers' training, in a variety of positions in divisional work, as training principal, and at territorial headquarters, we have tried to keep the weekday evening meal inviolate as not only a time for the family altar, but also as the focal point of sharing the day's activities, family fun, give and take. It is a time when we can get to know our children better and the children can get a chance to unwind and test the limits of their growing independence as they get to know their parents better.

Alice: Sometimes the impact of family standards is not realised until an unusual situation crops up. Some time ago we took grandpa out to a fancy old-English restaurant for a steak dinner to celebrate his 75th birthday. Several tables away, there were parents sharing a huge Hawaiian alcoholic drink with two straws. Their little girl, about seven years of age, was noticed by our then young son to stick her own straw into the glass and draw heavily upon the contents. His comment to us was, 'I don't think I like this restaurant.' 'What is wrong with it?' we asked. 'I think it is the wrong atmosphere!' he retorted. We were glad he was sensitive enough to notice something that, hopefully, would not be allowed in his own future home.

David: For this message to reach the widest possible group is a difficult assignment for we realise we are speaking through these pages to a broad cross-section of Salvation Army and Christian fellowship, to adherents of the Army and to non-salvationists. Some readers will have no children. Perhaps you are just starting out on marriage, but routines could be established and devotions could so easily be left out. We are speaking also to older couples with an 'empty nest' and this group may feel less of a necessity for family devotions. They may feel that this time has less meaning since all the children have left. For each of these groups, we believe, there can be a family altar as the focal point to holy living. Corporate worship around a table in the home can add immensely to the spiritual dimensions of one's life.

Alice: In preparing this chapter, we tried to draw upon as many resources as possible—from our experiences as Salvation Army officers, from our long years together, and from all the experiences

89

of the soldier and officer friends and other Christian people we have known and visited, some good and some bad.

David: I will never forget as a boy, the late Commissioner Samuel Hepburn, then a young major, our divisional commander and a great holiness exponent, who, after a late night 'battle for souls' in a salvation meeting, came often to our house. He would gather us all around the dining-room table, kick off his shoes, eat a bowl of cornflakes and then have us all kneel at our chairs. We would hear him fervently pour out his heart to God. It was hard for my parents to keep four unruly boys from pinching, punching or taking part in tomfoolery during those times of communication with Heaven, but it stands out as a highlight to me.

Alice: If it was hard to have family devotions with four boys, what do you think it was like with four giggling, mischief-filled girls when my parents tried to quieten us at the end of the meal? I must confess that there was the occasional time when my dad, the late Commissioner William Chamberlain, gave up in disgust as the laughter and nonsense became too raucous. He saw he was fighting a losing battle and gave in!

David: These diversions are true of any age. The first time I formally met my wife was when I was invited to dinner at the Chamberlain home in Pittsburgh, Pennsylvania, along with a young bandsman, and we all read our 'promise' from the *Bread of Life* holder and then the poetry on the back of the little card. Alas, the devotions came to a quick halt when David Appleby, the young bandsman, read this quaint little verse, 'I'm only a little sparrow . . .', to be followed by peals of laughter from four uncontrollable girls! Fun and laughter should be a main ingredient in any fellowship, particularly in the family setting.

Alice: There are many items of reading we have used down through the years. We had to change the styles as the children grew or as their needs called for it. There is a wealth of material, both Army and other Christian publications, and no one should feel they cannot find something suitable. Wise Christian publishers have tried to meet the need of every age.

David: Childhood is the time to instil reverence, respect for God's word and an appreciation of the family 'quiet time'. I cannot remember a day in my childhood, when I was leaving for school, that I did not see at least one or the other of my parents kneeling beside the bed to begin their day with God. Thus, my own personal devotions should become a natural part of my life, because I saw holiness and the spiritual life lived out by godly people in the lives of my mum and dad.

Alice: May I add that this is all reinforced in the mind of a child by much more than the 'quiet time' or personal devotions. If marriage is to be truly Christian and if it is to work, then it's your daily living and activities in and out of the home, your real and actual care and concern about your child's life in general that will count. Let me give you some examples. As a divisional guard director and later as home league secretary, it was my task to do a number of reviews and inspections and my son was not as resilient in coping with my absence as was my daughter. The moment he was off to school, I'd be off as fast as I could drive to get in the inspections and return before school came out at 3.30 pm, so I could greet him as he came through the door. This was not always possible where corps were four and five hours away, but we'd make these events weekend excursions or family fun trips.

David: My wife also has helped me to be a better father by each of us taking turns with all the children, whichever one of us was home, to make sure that not only were prayers said at bedtime, but a quiet sharing and understanding of the day and an interest in their life was shown. Does making my marriage truly Christian boil down in the end to my really caring? I must confess I thought of the pile of correspondence when I reluctantly went to school for parent/teacher meetings, visited cub pack programmes and concerts. It became worthwhile when I saw how much it meant to our children, Sue and David, to know we were in the audience and that we cared enough to be there. In Winston Churchill's memoirs, he couldn't understand at all why his personal physician flew from the company of famous men to be at his son's grammar school graduation, but I can understand. What we are simply trying to say, and we are saying it very simply, is that the period called 'family devotions' and referred to as a family altar, is but a small segment of the totality of life if a Christian marriage is to be effective in the home. The tone of a husband and wife relationship is important to a meaningful family altar. Bickering, squabbles and divisiveness do not make a good setting for the reading of God's word. Spiritual growth in the home can begin with a good family conference to make the children aware of the family needs, problems and burdens. To pin-point prayer power thus is to make it most effective.

Alice: We have tried to add one other dimension to this devotional life in making our marriage work. That is, we have prayed together in our bedroom every Sunday night throughout our married life. Can I hear someone say, 'once a week is not too much to boast about'. No, we cannot boast, but we felt it was a time to sum up the week with the Lord and begin the new week together.

David: It should be noted that in the use of all the fine devotional material available today, there is a tendency to read about the Bible instead of reading the Bible itself. Probably the best type of sample could be the style of *The Soldier's Armoury,* where a brief Bible reading by one member of the family and the commentary reading by another could be followed by short discussion or brief comments. *The Soldier's Armoury* is not always suitable for young children, but there is a children's edition that can be meaningful (*First Things First* by Heather Coutts). On the other hand, we should help our families to stretch their minds to the point of wanting more and deeper spiritual food. Just now I feel I've over-done it when I see my brand-new William Barclay devotional book, *Daily Celebration,* being carried off to college by my kids when I have just paid 7.50 dollars for it!

Alice: The use of family singing, Bible story records, sharing, relating to the day's activity, holding hands, forming a family circle around the table all add to meaningful family memories and instil a spirit of family unity. Much will depend on the ages of the children. Holidays can be a problem, but also times of special blessing.

David: We found as young corps officers, we were cheating our-selves and our people out of the spiritual gifts of Christmas when we allowed all we had to do (arranging kettles, organising workers, counting money and giving out Christmas baskets) to rob us of our personal enjoyment and spiritual development. So we started early and planned ahead.

Alice: We decorated the house early in the season for we saw it only at night time. The Advent wreath, with its four candles, one for each week in Advent, has become a spiritual as well as annual tradition and neither the Lord, the people, nor the family got 'left overs' from well-meaning but exhausted officers. The same busy pressures come to lay salvationists.

David: Our son, David, when he was four years old, prayed each month for six months: 'Thank God for Christmas all year long!' Thus, time and attention is given not only to holidays and birth-days, but to seasonal things like Thanksgiving, mother's and father's days, plus the whole gamut of the Christian calendar.

Alice: What we want to say is that the family altar and building each other up in the faith is not confined to family devotions and cannot be isolated into a 10-minute spot. It should be as natural and meaningful as eating a meal, part of our total day and life-style.

David: A cautionary note should remind us that the family altar is not a panacea to our family ills. There are many godly people, both officers and soldiers, throughout the Army world who have diligently prayed with and for their children and have not seen them show any spiritual leanings in their lifetime. Let us not be too quick to criticise when the children do not follow the footsteps of their Christlike parents. In the end, a child must make up his own mind about the gospel. But in the home, we are constantly making memories. Our main task, as salvationist parents, is to lead our children to Christ, to develop in them a spiritual sensitivity and awareness, to awaken in them responses which will help them in facing up to the harshness of life in a secular, sometimes amoral world. In this, every memory of home plays its part.

12

Some practical thoughts about Salvation Army family life

Captain and Mrs Ted and Dianne Palmer (Canada)

LIKE the priest and the Levite in the Good Samaritan parable, salvationists are very busy in religious activity. Unfortunately, that busyness can become a spiritual stumbling block rather than an opportunity. We can become people who, in rushing off to corps events and sharing in charitable activities, fail to accept our God-given responsibility to meet a need in the life of a near neighbour. Such a sin of omission is particularly horrendous when that neighbour is the spouse, child, or parent that God has given us.

The Salvation Army has activities for everyone in the family. However, most of those activities are spread over six nights of the week and each one involves only a fraction of the family. Daughters may go to brownies and guides on Monday, mother to the home league meeting on Tuesday, the youngest children to a junior soldiers' meeting on Wednesday, sons and teens to cubs and corps cadets on Thursday, dad to do his *War Cry* distribution on Friday and some to youth and other Army activities on Saturday. This walk through a typical week doesn't even include the mid-week Bible study or house meeting, band, songster, singing company and timbrel practices. Weeks like this could tend to fragment rather than strengthen family life.

It will never be possible to eliminate all those corps activities that are defined by the age, sex, or function of the participant. Even in corps situations where a real effort is made to consolidate weekday activities in order to enhance family life, there will still be some pressure from events which, though valuable in terms of corps life and ministry, are an unhealthy intrusion into an already fragile family circle.

Although most contemporary Christians experience this centrifugal pressure to a certain degree, it can often be intense in The Salvation Army. By definition, we are a movement that communicates the gospel through practical good deeds. We pride ourselves on doing a lot for others, and others have come to expect a lot of us. Because of this, salvationist parents who try to master— rather than be enslaved by—their timetables, are often afflicted with a false guilt. 'Don't you care?' a little voice keeps saying. 'So many people out there who need to be saved; so many who need to be helped! Are you going to stay at home just to be with your family?' Yet the voice of God exhorts us through Scripture: 'But if any provide not for his own, and specially for those of his own house, he hath denied the faith, and is worse than an infidel' (1 Timothy 5:8).

How easy it is to get our priorities wrong, to bow to the external demands imposed by both the well-meaning and the malicious, and make the voice of God of secondary significance. Musical excellence, impressive attendances, and a full corps programme may be important goals. But they are not as important as personal and family spirituality. They constitute a real and necessary, but secondary, motivation in the Christian life. A day to day walking in the Spirit (Romans 8:1) in our family life should be the primary 'pressure'. To fail in this area rightly results in *real* guilt.

Salvationist parents must make objective evaluations and seek the Holy Spirit's wisdom (James 1:5) in responding to the unintentional but intense pressure created by the corps programme. Through a clear grasp of priorities, a healthy balance must be struck between ministry within and to the family and that without and through the family: 'every home should be as definitely and truly consecrated to the service of God as the Salvation Army hall. It should be a temple where he is loved and worshipped, and in which he can reveal himself. . . .' (William Booth in *Marriage and Home*, 1902).

This commitment to family spirituality, based on the principle of loving one's near neighbour (Luke 10:27), implies an obligation to serve, as a Christian family, those in our immediate community. Family life is not an escape from ministry, but rather a more integrated response to it.

For example, some holidays are still actually 'holy days', particularly Christmas and Easter. Those living near us, who see us coming and going in our Salvation Army uniforms, not only anticipate some input from us, they positively hope for it! How disappointed they must be when we run out to the car night after night in December and drive across town to sing Christmas carols and distribute the special issue of *The War Cry*! Here is an appropriate time for our family, as a family, to visit the homes nearest us, taking along an Army publication, a seasonal tract and a sincere 'God loves you!' If you have enough musical talent in your family, you might even give your neighbours the gift of a couple of carols. Easter, with newspaper, radio and television emphasis on pilgrimages to the Holy Land, and the availability of another seasonal issue of *The War Cry,* is also an opportunity for a timely word. It is particularly a time for your family, as a family, to share its faith with the neighbours.

Similarly, your home can be a league of mercy outpost, assuming a ministry to elderly or sick people on your street who lack strong families and are not church members. You might take turns reading the Scriptures to someone with impaired vision; your family could—as a group—look after the spring cleaning for a disabled person; a couple of you might do the washing while others scrub down the shelves or vacuum the floors. The recipient of these 'favours' will certainly be blessed. But your family will also benefit for they will sense that this ministry was not designed by the Army, but was rather a direct leading by the Holy Spirit to them as a family.

Service and outreach, family to family style, might include such low-key evangelism as camping trips, picnics and special meals with those in the neighbourhood. If such social contacts are preceded by genuine prayer within the family circle, then everyone in your home will be clear about and committed to the spiritual intention involved. The Early Church was a 'home industry': '. . . breaking bread *from house to house,* did eat their meat with gladness and singleness of heart, praising God, and having favour with all the people. And the Lord added to the church daily such as should be saved' (Acts 2:46, 47) (italics added).

As a family, we can also make evangelistic forays into the larger community. Salvationist parents and children could hold their own open-air meetings, some being able to contribute musical skills. How good for the children to see their dad as a salvation platoon commander. How good for mum to support dad and to be an example to her children in Scripture reading and testimony! How good for each son and daughter to be an integral part of a family outreach, through his or her playing, singing and personal sharing!

Salvationist families are often trained and experienced in the skills required to conduct meetings in senior citizens' complexes and chronic care hospitals. It is very fulfilling to be part of a one-family league of mercy brigade. In addition, the interest of the congregation in such places can be captivated more quickly when they are aware that it is a family unit that is ministering to them.

Some of the physical work relating to the delivery of Christmas hampers can be appropriately done by families. Instead of bemoaning the fact that mum has been down at the Army for five nights putting together hampers, why not take all the members of your family for one night of intensive work together. Such an experience can be enhanced by your sharing an inexpensive restaurant meal together beforehand or by stopping off for a treat on the way home.

There are, however, many ways to serve God as a family without ever leaving home. Self-denial gifts can be more than just a matter of dad writing a special cheque on the Sunday of the altar service. The whole family can get involved in fund-raising by, for example:

> 'paying' for each hour of television viewed; giving up all desserts and watching mum put a definite amount of money (representing the cost of the desserts that they would have had) into a conspicuous container in the middle of the table; hiring out as a group to paint fences, clean up an orchard, or pick strawberries.

Letter-writing can be a family affair. One hour devoted to such Christian service can be very productive and rewarding. Letters assuring them of prayer support can be written to various missionaries. Correspondence to editors of newspapers and magazines on moral issues such as pornography, abortion, war and euthanasia can be a real way of 'salting' our community. Similarly, letters of support or protest to government officials or your political representatives can assist those in authority in assessing the correctness of their present direction. Each letter should stick to the issue at hand, share clearly the relevant scriptural principle (including Bible verses) and be written in a respectful tone. We want to influence issues, but we also want to win people.

A family might be involved in the parents' calling to Salvation Army officer-service or to a short-term commitment as a lay ministering team. When discerning the guidance of the Holy Spirit at such times, it is important to listen to what *all* members of the family are saying about the proposed step. A definite reluctance or sustained rebelliousness toward such a 'call' may be a sign that the timing is not right.

What we do and how we do it are as much our message as the words we speak and sing. When people see our family witnessing and serving as *a family unit,* they receive the following two messages:

1 God's reality is not confined to those activities that a denomination organises and directs.

2 God is not an enemy of family life, but rather one who has worked through families both to bless them and also to challenge others.

'And if it seem evil unto you to serve the Lord, choose you this day whom ye will serve . . . but *as for me and my house, we will serve the Lord*' (Joshua 24:15) (italics added).

There is great joy in such family ministry. Indeed, salvationists who establish the right priorities, balancing their ministry in the corps with a valid and vital ministry in and through the family, possess a potential for happiness envied by those outside our ranks. It can be fun to be a Salvation Army family! In The Salvation Army are opportunities for doing things together and a level of liveliness that few other Christian expressions can equal.

Sunday is a busy day for Army families, but it can be enjoyable. Starting the day with a special family breakfast helps to establish a positive atmosphere. The Sunday main meal should be a highlight of the week. Looking forward to better fare than usual, perhaps even with a favourite dessert, fosters a pleasant anticipation! Fasting, properly understood and properly undertaken, is a definite aid to the spiritual life, but Sunday is a feast-day, a day on which we remember the resurrection of our Lord Jesus Christ. The Old Testament Sabbath was rather austere and confining. The Christian 'first day of the week' is a celebration!

In addition to the sensuous delights of feasting, Sunday can be a great time of Christian fellowship for each family that constitutes a part of the congregational 'family of God'. Such fellowship is enhanced the more the family operates as a unit. In addition to attending meetings together, family members should make a special point of supporting each other at knee-drill, open-air meetings and visitation outreach. The more the family functions as an intact unit, the greater will be their experience of 'pleasure in his service'. The more Sunday becomes a series of 'solo flights' the greater will be the sense of frustration and disenchantment. Any team has more fun when all its members are at the game, and in the .game!

Army families can have a special experience of family joy as they take time for special spiritual meetings in their own home and confined to their family circle. Each home should indeed be a little citadel of witness to those without and sanctification to those within. God's exhortation to family heads saying, 'thou shalt teach them [God's laws] diligently unto thy children, and shalt talk of them when thou *sittest in thine house,* and when thou walkest by the way, and when thou liest down, and when thou risest up' (Deuteronomy 6:7) (italics added) focuses very much on the home setting. There is here, of course, a most serious responsibility. But there is as well the potential for a tremendous joy—that of being a pastor who contributes to the spiritual development of one's own children.

In addition to supper-time devotions and/or morning prayers, numerous salvationist families are now enjoying a 'family at home night' together. They see now that both their involvement in Sunday and weekday meetings in the corps and community, and the hours they spend together in the intimacy of their home, should be equally consecrated to God.

A 'family at home night' can be a lot of fun. Playing a favourite game, enjoying a special snack, laughing and clapping through an informal sing-song, or playing a family game of soccer in a nearby park can all contribute to this one night a week when everybody stays at home. The evening can conclude with a short Bible study, chorus singing, sharing and prayer time. Few joys surpass those which can arise out of these times:

- —hearing a child ask forgiveness of a brother or sister;
- —praying for dad after he's shared a problem he's facing at work;
- —leading a son or daughter to salvation with the living-room couch as the mercy seat with dad or mum as the counsellor;
- —joining hands and singing 'We are one in the Spirit';
- —having a son share that he first responded to the challenge of holiness during a family spiritual time.

Dedications, enrolments, weddings, commissionings and funerals can be precious family times that Army folk can enjoy. Our involvement in the life of the corps doesn't prevent times of rich human fellowship. In fact, it gives us some extra excuses for getting together! Such events involve a double pleasure: that of meeting with each other and that of introducing family and friends to our Saviour, Jesus Christ. What a thrill it is for a family to know that, through an after-dedication party or an after-the-swearing-in reception, a loved one has come to know the Lord. After someone's promotion to Glory (the Army expression for the death of a salvationist) there is time for rejoicing, as when a member of the family is given secular promotion.

The Salvation Army, due to its colourful style and the frequent special gatherings, provides an unsurpassed opportunity for family fun times: there is, indeed, 'joy in The Salvation Army'.

A recent development in some territories has increased the possibility of experiencing that joy as a family unit. Scheduling a number of activities on a single night rather than spreading them throughout numerous week nights, these family nights at the corps encourage the families to come *as families* for mid-week activities.

Such an evening can commence with young people's activities, directly after school. These might include timbrels, the young people's band, cubs and brownies. When, later, dad and mum have arrived at the corps, they contribute a casserole or plate of cheese to the pot-luck meal that then gets under way. Each family sits together in a large room as God's family in that corps. After a co-operative effort at clean-up, various Bible study groups get under way, including junior soldiers and corps cadets. Later different groups form for music practices, home league, scouts and guides. At the end of the evening, the corps officer gathers all the families together for a brief Bible meditation and prayer.

It takes time and a real spirit of co-operation to develop this sort of family night. But it is well worth the effort to see families together as intact units for one night a week at the corps. One of the loveliest and quietly-happy experiences a corps can have can come at the end of such an evening when, after the corps officer's Bible meditation and his sharing of some crucial concerns, each family forms a little circle of prayer and its members take turns talking to God. 'Blest be the tie that binds our hearts in Christian love' has a dual meaning and a multiplied joy as the families are in one accord in prayer.

Beyond all the bits and pieces of programme at the corps and organisation within the home is the happy satisfaction in knowing for sure that we are saved and serving Jesus in his Army.

Every corps officer, local officer and parent has a personal responsibility to develop and maintain a proper balance between the spirituality of the home and the work and witness of the corps. But, having been faithful to that crucial responsibility, they will find that there are few more effective channels for Christian growth and usefulness for their family than the ranks of The Salvation Army.

Part Four
We believe in marriage

Let us go deeper
you and I
for we belong together
and love's image dwells within
God's you and I;
we must explore in prayer
and find the real each other,
awareness growing all the time
for each is for the other
in the likeness of Christ's mind.

Exploration into Love, Malling Abbey, 1970.
(Quoted in *Marriage, Divorce and the Church,* SPCK, 1971.)

13

Anna and Freddy
Major and Mrs Münch (Congo)

NOW that our three children are old enough to marry, and realise the importance of marriage, we are challenged to think over our personal experience and our vision of married life.

How have we lived? What is the worth of the example we have given? What can we tell them? And what can we tell young people of our days?

This is the story of our love. . . .

Anna: As far as I can remember, my parents were united, happy people. They were a harmonious couple. In eastern fashion (I am of Armenian extraction) my father worked to earn the daily bread for his large family of seven children, whereas our mother was really the mother of the home; always there for each of us, watching, listening, thinking, laughing. . . . She was the soul of the family.

Our home was hospitable, open to all and at every hour. I wonder if there has ever been a key on the door . . . which remained open day and night!

My parents were true, committed Christians and consistent with their faith. It was as I witnessed their lives that I learned what 'love for thy neighbour' meant; a life of prayer, a life of faith. My parents experienced many miracles and we shared that life of victory. They had the gift to turn our eyes away from trials and difficulties (and we had many!) to show us the wonderful way which God was to use to get us out of 'this scrape'!

At the end of our street there was on the right the Armenian Evangelical Church and, on the left, the Salvation Army hall. We used to go into one of these on Sunday and the other one on Thursday; so we were growing in a real Christian atmosphere. Everything in our lives was seen, judged and realised in that perspective: first of all God's will. At the age of nine we suffered bombing raids and my parents lost all their material goods (they had previously lost everything in Turkey); the house was fissured from top to bottom but . . . we were all alive! I can see my parents, their eyes full of tears, thanking God for having kept us alive. It was at that time that I was converted and at the same time received my call to be a Salvation Army officer (I had thus opted for the left side of the street!).

If we loved our father tremendously, it was with mum that we were able to share our life. She understood all our feelings and she knew perfectly what to tell us to help us. She opened our eyes about happy married couples, helping us to see the reasons for their happiness: same aim, same ideal, same faith, same social environment; a life oriented towards others. She taught us the vanity of living for money, the vanity of a self-centred married life. In that way there grew in my heart the strong desire to build a united happy home. I remember well that day when I said to mum, 'You see, God calls me to be an Army officer but I cannot envisage a single life!' Mum answered, 'Well! Put your confidence in God. He created you and he called you. He knows what you need and he will give you the best.' Today I know that my husband is the best!

I had some fixed principles concerning my intended husband: he should not only have the same calling as I had, but he should also love his mother and not criticise her (I still believe that a young man who loves his mother will love his wife too).

At the age of 18 I went to the national camp for youth at Le Chambon-sur-Lignon in France. There in our team was Freddy Münch. Son of salvationists, he loved the Lord and wanted to serve him. Our camp lasted two weeks. I remember that when we parted (there was between us just a nice friendship) I got the certainty that if Freddy would become an officer it was he that God had chosen for me! Therefore I awaited God's hour in a spirit of prayer. Five years later Freddy made a short stay in Paris before leaving for Cameroun where he was to work. It was again in a youth camp that we met and there Freddy asked me to be his wife. He knew that he had to be a Salvation Army officer and he was willing to obey fully but he was leaving for Cameroun in order to test his calling. He was eager to know if it was his inclination for adventure or a real call of God which was challenging him to go overseas. It was easy for me to agree with his calling; a common life in God's service in the Army in Africa.

Freddy: When I think again of what was for me our home, I see my parents (who have been promoted to Glory) as a happy, united married couple. Very often I was conscious that it was not the same in every family and that I had—with my two sisters—a great privilege. I have never heard my parents quarrelling. My mother had rather frail health; therefore, when my father came home from his work, he would help her a lot, washing or rinsing heavy household linen, for example. This was the model we had before our eyes.

My parents were very different from one another. My mother liked to express her ideas—well-fixed ideas!—and showed that she had a high ideal of life. My father, on the contrary, spoke very little; he had a deep sense of the realities of life . . . with him everything was calculated and planned. However, once he had decided something, he was going to see his idea through!

Concerning religion, God had the first place, but my parents did not mention his name very often. There was a certain reserve but also the desire not to impose on us. Still, we were living in his presence. As children we learned Bible stories on our mother's knee and we were accustomed to going to Sunday-school, but family prayers were never compulsory. On the other hand great events of the year like Christmas, the wedding anniversary of our parents, birthdays of the children, were well celebrated and between 'cheese and dessert' appeared Bible and song-books; in our parents' prayer everyone was presented to God. We realised then that our parents had a true life with God.

They had been officers for five years, but because of the frail health of my mother (officers were leading a life of privation in France at that time) they left the ranks of officership to start again after the war as sergeant-major and sergeant in the corps at Strasbourg. I believe that they have been exemplary salvationists. Concerning their marriage our parents never told us: 'Look at us!' It was not their way of doing things, but my mother with whom we were used to speaking always told us, 'My children you must pray concerning your partner. God knows what you need. Put your confidence in him.' Therefore, at the time of my adolescence and for several years, I prayed for this. Not organised prayer meetings! No! But when I was walking, on the way to school or from school, I prayed from time to time.

When I met Anna in a Bible camp at the age of 18, I thought, 'This is a sensational girl!' We were good friends but then the idea of marriage was far away from me. This was because I felt young, I was finishing my studies, still without a stable situation, not knowing yet where my agricultural training would lead me, and facing my military obligations. But I must say that afterwards, when I thought of all the young girls I knew, it was always Anna who was the greatest . . . but maybe I was dreaming; perhaps it was too high a goal to see my future with her. . . .

I knew that she had a vocation to become an officer; as for me, I had been aware of God's call since I was 12 years of age. (I was converted in a campaign at Le Chambon-sur-Lignon where we stayed as war refugees.) Very quickly the idea of a missionary calling was developing in my mind, under I don't know what kind of influence. But the question was: 'The person who will be my wife, will she be willing to follow me? Will Anna accept the missionary adventure?' Until that time we did not write letters to each other: she was in Paris, I was in Strasbourg, with 500 km between us!

I was also well aware that to be able to marry I had to have a job, be able to do something valuable. For that reason after my military obligations I had a contract with the Ministry of Agriculture to serve in Cameroun which was then a French colony. I was 23 and it was time to apply my mind to the future. Before my departure for Cameroun, I had to stay in Paris at the Tropical Agricultural School and there, during a weekend for young people, I made my declaration to Anna. It was a great moment! Would Anna say 'yes'? 'Yes' to being my wife, but also 'yes' to Africa? If I dared to hope for a 'yes' to the first question (because there are certain signs which do not cheat!), I was not really sure about the second question. But she said 'yes, yes!' I sighed with relief! What thankfulness towards God in my heart!

We became engaged to each other . . . and to our families too. A mother, more brothers and sisters; it was indeed a very emotional time. This also is an important part of married life: one 'marries' also the family of the beloved.

Anna: I was presented to the family in Alsace . . . and we were engaged. Some days later, Freddy left for two years in the Cameroun. We shared all our days, our thoughts, our yearnings, our dreams . . . through letters! We shared also our love for God, the revelations of his word. The harmony between us was (and still is) perfect. There was only one shadow on the picture: the date of our wedding. We were already 25! If we had to wait on the training college and then two years after the commissioning (at that time it was the regulation; one could not marry before training in France!) it was really too long. Freddy wrote to headquarters in Paris to ask for an authorisation to be married before entering the training college. It was refused because of the regulations! But our application being a missionary one, our case was conveyed to London where the then International Secretary for Europe (Commissioner Norman Duggins) said, 'These two young people, what are they waiting for? If they marry now they will be able to go sooner to Africa!'

On 22 June 1957, Commissioner Charles Péan, who had just been appointed territorial commander in France, led the wedding ceremony asking God's blessing on our marriage.

Of that day I remember only the joy, the tenderness and love of all our friends who came to be with us and to congratulate us. More than 300 people filled the Central Hall in Paris. No, I cannot say anything else concerning my feelings about that day, or about the ceremony. I had prepared myself with seriousness, in worship and prayer, but that day there was only joy and such an overwhelming joy that I thought it would suffocate me! Then we had two-and-a-half months of honeymoon before entering the training college for Salvation Army officers.

'If one has found a good recipe, one keeps it even if one adds some other ingredients.' Today, our happiness is obvious and our children are aware of the fact. All three are now grown up: 24, 22 and 20 this year. All three have said that they would like to build a home as happy and as harmonious as ours. Our children have seen also how we have lived our married life in the ministry.

Then, we encourage our children to pray that God may give them the partner that he has chosen for them. We have often explained to them that a well-understood marriage is complete harmony, a spiritual, moral, intellectual, cultural and physical harmony. This last is wished and desired by God, but to see marriage as only a sexual union means to fail to obtain perfect harmony. When understanding is complete and when we pray to God for his blessing within the marriage, then he also gives as a last present, physical, sexual harmony; this is certainly not the least, but wonderfully completes the other points. We give advice to our children and we pray for them but their choice is not an easy one in the sort of world in which they are living. If they follow the Christian way, they are able to maintain an ideal towards marriage. If they reject God there are no more reasons to fight against the stream of so-called liberty which confronts our young people today.

Our married and family life has been lived mostly in the Congo. The fact that we are salvationists has been absolutely no constraint in the brightness of our loves and in our children's lives. The Salvation Army here is respected and our children have not suffered from mockery because they belonged to an Army family (as is sometimes the case in France). God called us, and those that he gave to us, in The Salvation Army and we are happy in this obedience. We taught our children to love the Army and to be thankful for all that the Army allowed us to experience in our family: openness to the world, true values in life, service for the neighbour, Christian family life, music and so on. Thus we tried to give them what seems to us to be of prime importance in life so that they could choose with the benefit of inside information.

Twenty-five years now. . . . Joy and euphoria have taken in my life another shape, deeper, stronger. . . . An always greater tenderness for my husband fills my heart and also a great respect when I see the rightness of his Christian life in each moment of his existence; the brightness that his love brought in my life as bride, mother and officer. These three sides of my life have never been divided, thanks to the attitude of my husband who has always respected my calling and who let me live my vocation with him.

Twenty-five years of real sharing: without doubt it is the secret of our conjugal happiness; of mutual respect and attentions for each other; of mutual forgiveness for so many small wounds, never really heavy when love is covering them; giving our home for others, for all those who come to us, who need its warmth. Considering all this, I would still choose marriage today!

Freddy: To my wife's reflections (with which I fully agree) I would like to add this: to be married is in fact something extraordinary. Until then, one has lived in one's own way, one thinks and works alone, according to one's own ideas, influenced by one's education and experiences. And now one must take account of the other—the partner—who has his or her own nature, own experience, own education, own way of life. The problem in a couple is the art of becoming one, to be complementary. For some people it is easier than for others. As far as Anna and I are concerned, there was a great difference in our natures and also in our religious and salvationist experience: she is of Eastern extraction, Armenian, with all that it means in exuberance, speaking easily, joy of life, hospitality and availability to others.

For me, a continental, reserved, rather silent and uncommunicative man, choosing my friends carefully, marriage was really a tornado in my life! But since we were only one, I adapted myself, but it was not always easy! Again, Anna was a committed salvationist for many years and she became an officer heartily. For me, it was a more difficult adjustment; to become an officer was for me an act of obedience, not one of personal taste. Thus our marriage could have failed because of our unlikeness, but it became strong because we shared everything, speaking together about our differences.

Our greatest wish was and still is that our married life be a witness for God's glory and be useful for our ministry, for our children, for our friends and now for our cadets in the officers' training college here in Brazzaville.

For discussion

Anna and Freddy are very different personalities. Do you think this is often the case in marriage and that there is an attraction of opposites? What kind of conflicts might arise and have to be resolved?

(See the Subject Index under *adapting to one another.*)

14

Shigeko and Jinichi

Young People's Sergeant-Major and Mrs Osato
(Japan)

JESUS CHRIST gives meaning and joy to family life. To this fact, my wife and children and I bear witness. Although we are very ordinary people, we are amazed to see how Christ brought us together and guides us according to his good purpose. This is all the more remarkable when we consider our background. Let me speak on behalf of my family.

In my young adulthood, I was made aware of the tragedy of broken marriage relationships. This instilled a sense of caution in my mind. In 1960 a friend introduced a woman to me about whom I knew nothing previously. Gradually we had fellowship together in order to get to know each other's character and understand our respective philosophies of life. This woman's name was Shigeko and I was horrified to discover that she was a Christian. To add to my shock, I learned that this woman and her family were soldiers of The Salvation Army. At that time I was completely indifferent toward Christianity. In fact, I really thought that the teachings of Buddha were much more suited to the Japanese people and that Buddhism was more in harmony with Japanese culture than Christianity. However, I was not really a Buddhist. I neither accepted nor denied any religion.

In visiting Shigeko's home I felt a warm and loving atmosphere which was different from my own home where there was no particular religion. There a peaceful heart was my experience and I felt it was because this family was cultivated in the Christian faith. During our courtship, Shigeko and I felt more closely drawn together and meant for each other. We came to the decision that we would like to marry. When I proposed to Shigeko and sought her parents' approval of our marriage, they asked if I would agree to a Christian marriage ceremony in Kiryu Corps. Whilst I did not feel particularly comfortable with this thought, I did not hesitate to

109

agree so long as they accepted the fact that I was not a Christian nor had any thought of becoming one. My own parents did not oppose either our marriage or the selected location for the ceremony even though they knew nothing about Christianity and less about The Salvation Army. They associated no great importance to the type or location of the marriage ceremony. As I look back on this experience, I can understand how this was the beginning of Christ's guidance to bring me to himself and to create a Christian home.

The Christian ceremony was actually quite nice and the salvationists were very kind to me. After our marriage my wife invited me to attend with her the meetings of the Kiryu Corps. Since I did not mind doing this for her, we rode our bicycles to the Sunday meetings in the corps. It was difficult for me to understand the Christian messages in the holiness and salvation meetings. This was only natural since I knew nothing about Jesus Christ and had never read the Christian Bible. Because attending the meetings seemed to please my new bride and the people at the Army were so warm and friendly, I continued to attend. The joyous and holy atmosphere of this corps gave to me a sense of peace of heart. However, it was not easy for me to commit myself to Jesus Christ and to believe in him fully. I had been a member of a university Buddhist study group which had greatly influenced me. I became an elementary school teacher and found myself still interested in, and attached to, Buddhist philosophy. So there was a real conflict of faith in my heart and I could not easily become converted to Christ.

Later in 1961 our son, Tadahiro, was born. My wife asked me to agree to a Christian dedication ceremony at the Salvation Army corps. I was not too enthusiastic about this idea but since it was my wife's strong desire I followed her will and our son was dedicated to God in the Kiryu Corps. Because our son was now dedicated to the Christian God, I thought it was proper that he be cultivated in the Christian faith.

I continued to attend the Christian meetings at the corps and when our daughter, Kyoko, was born four years later, we had her dedication ceremony at the corps also. Gradually I learned more about the Christian faith. I was impressed with my wife's Christian life which was marked by kind consideration and quiet joy.

The cadets from the officers' training college campaigned in our corps in November 1968. We were requested to billet two women cadets. I did not object. These young women invaded our home with joyous enthusiasm and personal interest. Their lives were so wholesome and I was moved by their wholehearted devotion to

God and The Salvation Army. They campaigned very hard but when they returned to our home at night, though they were tired, they were overflowing with joy and gave glowing accounts of their opportunities and victories. I see now that this too was part of Christ's leading and prevenient work of grace in my life. I was convicted in my heart because I had been rather passively attending the corps with my wife, but here were young Christians full of enthusiasm for God's service. They were serious and sincere. This caused me to more seriously and decisively consider becoming a real Christian believer. I accepted Christ as my Saviour and began to follow the Christian way. My wife all the while was patient, understanding and helpful in guiding me into the Christian life. We are each individuals with differing backgrounds but God led us together and now that God was the centre of our home we could experience true family happiness.

Although we live busy lives and the demands of my profession, with increasing responsibility, have been very heavy, we continue the habit of keeping the Lord's day and spending Sunday at the Army. We assist with the Sunday-school. My daughter is now the corps organist and my son, now in his third year of university working on an education degree, is also the leader of the divisional youth evangelistic group. It is a real joy to see him so active for Christ. As a family we attend the holiness meeting together. We enjoy family worship together in our home which is pervaded with a happy, peaceful atmosphere. We discuss problems together but do not experience quarrels because we have a sense of unity and love in Jesus Christ. He is Lord of our home and our lives.

It has not been easy for me to wear Salvation Army uniform in public. I had a very strange feeling the first time I donned the uniform and was seen in the streets of the city where I am so well known because of my profession. But I gained the victory and am happy to wear the uniform as a distinguishing mark of a Christian and a serving salvationist. We are now a uniformed family. God gives us each many opportunities to 'let our light shine!'

My wife, Shigeko, is the home league welcome sergeant and I am the young people's sergeant-major in the corps. We believe in giving the Lord his proper share of our income and have been blessed in this.

In my present position as Deputy Chief of the Special Education Department for the City of Kiryu and Consultant to School Teachers, I have a specific opportunity to deal with behavioural problems that result largely from broken homes or domestic disharmony. Not only teachers come to me for consultation on student-teacher problems, but many parents seek me out for counsel. My own strong family relationships which are Christian-oriented, give me a sense of confidence in offering guidance professionally to those desiring domestic tranquillity and corrective guidance for their young people. Opportunities are mine also to speak and write on the subjects of family in crisis, building a strong family unit in society, counter-measures for juvenile delinquency and improving inter-human relationships. I have just reviewed a book dealing with some of these issues for the *Territorial Home League Quarterly* in Japan.

Recently there has been a steady increase in divorce and broken homes in Japan. In many instances where the home is not broken, the families are divided and cannot get along together. Youths who have no clear goals in life resort to misconduct. This accounts for the increase of juvenile delinquency and schoolroom violence in Japan. These conditions present us all with great challenges and none more than the Christian family. We have a responsibility to reach these families and individuals who desperately need God's salvation and Christ's presence in their homes and individual lives. Therefore, salvationist families who have discovered the secret of happiness in God-centred homes must increasingly give witness to this joy and harmony which God has bestowed—to Japanese society in general and to their given communities in particular.

Shigeko and I are most grateful to God and The Salvation Army for these past 22 years of happy family life with its God-glorifying purpose and Christian service opportunities. We can heartily recommend in the midst of our modern materialistic and spiritually confused Japanese society the Christ-guided family life available to all through our wonderful Lord and Saviour Jesus Christ.

For discussion

Here, only one partner was a salvationist or even a Christian. Discuss how Jinichi was gradually won to the Lord. What are your thoughts about marrying someone who does not share your faith?

(See the Subject Index under *marrying a non-Christian*.)

15

Rashidan and Emmanuel

Major and Mrs Iqbal (Pakistan)

I WAS born into an Army family and my parents named me Emmanuel, meaning 'God with us'. I enjoyed growing in a Salvation Army atmosphere and it was in the Army boys' hostel that I became converted. At the age of 13 I was stricken deaf and dumb, and praying to God I promised to give him my all if only he would heal me. Within three months I was completely well. At that time I was a corps cadet and became a company guard, teaching in the Sunday-school, later on.

Passing my matriculation examination, I thought it would be good to become a teacher, then, remembering my promises to God, I applied to the Candidates' Department. They were prepared to accept me for Salvation Army officership provided I married! Now I had never thought of marriage amongst my plans and I certainly had no one in mind, so in this matter I turned to my father for help. He asked if I would be prepared to accept his choice of a wife for me and, thinking of the story of Isaac and Rebekah, I agreed.

My father visited a family who belonged to the United Presbyterian Church, but who sometimes visited The Salvation Army. This family were very surprised at the purpose of his visit, but their young daughter agreed to the negotiations for our marriage as she too accepted the wisdom of her parents. Eventually we were both accepted for training in the Courageous Session in 1957. Even then, we were not married and had not even seen each other!

Our marriage date was fixed for 6 July 1957. The ceremony and feast arrangements were all made. The bridegroom's party went to the bride's home and the divisional commander conducted the ceremony. It is difficult to write of the emotions of that day, especially when you do not know your partner, but God helped us for he had called us both. It is not really necessary to 'know' but to accept that you both have now become 'one body', feeling the joys and pains of living with and for each other. So our marriage day was one of rejoicing in the Lord. Three days after our marriage we were in the training college and thus we accepted the challenge of building a Christian home founded upon love, nourished and strengthened by it.

As we look back upon our family life, we find that we always tried, and still try, to care for each other. One never forces their opinions on the other. We have no secrets and we talk to each other openly and frankly. If there is something that we cannot agree on, we try to compromise so we get better results. If there is a family concern, we think about it and discuss it together so that the problem is shared.

Although our parents chose us for each other, we look back over our 26 years of happy married life and praise God for successful goals reached as a family. Because we live in a society where children have faith in the choice of partner by their parents, we shall be doing the same for our family. Western customs are so different from ours and we may seem to be foolish, but we don't have so many divorces! When our children see our marriage working successfully they will raise no objection as to our choice which will be wisely made on their behalf. On the other hand, if they want to make their own choice, they will surely consult with us and because we trust them I am sure that we can happily agree to their choice.

I would advise any salvationist that if you want to enjoy a happy and successful married life, never cease your daily family devotions. Never speak of The Salvation Army in a destructive way before your children but try to speak in a constructive way. 'And whatsoever ye do in word or deed, do all in the name of the Lord Jesus . . .' (Colossians 3:17), then God will bless you and your family.

For discussion

Rashidan and Emmanuel's marriage was arranged for them by their parents. This is the custom in some cultures and amongst certain immigrant communities in the west. What do you think about it? What contribution can family attitudes make to the stability or otherwise of any marriage?

(See the Subject Index under *relatives*.)

16

Freda and John
Lieut-Colonel and Mrs Larsson (Chile)

She writes
I WAS brought up in the home of officer-parents and saw for many
years a happy and fulfilled marriage, which gave me a good basis
on which to build my own future.

As a single officer in my late 20s I had really settled for the fact
that this would be the pattern of my future, when unexpectedly
things changed.

John and I had known each other for about five years when at a
residential councils for officers we met for a business discussion
connected with his first musical, *Takeover Bid*. As we talked we
discovered an affinity of ideas and feelings on other subjects as
well, and before the end of the councils we were meeting on a more
personal basis. It was the beginning of what proved to be a brief
courtship. Our hearts, minds and spirits told us that our future lay
together, and on 5 July 1969 we were married.

Marriage is one of God's choicest blessings—and it is a blessing
that grows. Looking back, the first year was a year of adjustment.
Together with the excitement of a new relationship came the
demands of getting used to each other's ways—and I found I had to
get used to the idea of sharing my husband with the many corps
folk claiming his attention.

But such adjustments were by far outweighed by the joy of
having that one person with whom I could share my innermost
feelings, thoughts and ideals, in my daily life and work and in my
spiritual life. It is the kind of relationship I have never shared with
anyone else. What a joy it is to have a relationship that makes us
completely relaxed with each other. It is a constant factor in the
ever-changing life of officership which is ours. It makes a home of
the succession of houses we have lived in, and enables not only us,
but our children as well, to enjoy the security of a happy family
life.

We sometimes feel awed by the responsibility of the upbringing of our two children—aged 11 and 10 at the time of writing. We try to give them a wide and varied experience of life as we seek to guide and help them in their physical, mental and spiritual growth.

We truly thank the Lord for each other and the deep relationship he has given us to share.

He continues

Without perhaps ever formulating it in words or even as a specific thought, one of the foremost longings with respect to marriage when I was a young single officer was to find a partner who would be a true home-maker, so that together we might establish a secure family life with parents and children bound together by bonds of love and affection. In this my ideals were without doubt influenced by the happy home circumstances I had known as a child. In Freda I found such a life-partner.

Again, without ever sitting down and consciously mapping out a plan, it would seem, as we look back over our years of marriage, that the idea of balance has been important to us.

For example, we have sought to achieve a balance with regard to our respective officer-roles. Though, with our young children, Freda's main role has been in the home, we have tried to arrange things between us so that at no time would she be cut off from specific officer-responsibilities. Whatever our appointments, Freda has always had a part of that appointment or some other Army responsibility which was her 'own thing'—and we have tried to organise our time so that when she had to be out I would be home.

The same seems to have applied with regard to our children. Fortunately, helped by two very co-operative boys, we have tried to achieve a balance between exposing them to their parents' Army life and protecting them in the family setting. When we were corps officers, Freda frequently did her visiting pushing a pram—or with two boys in the back seat of the car. When a change of appointment involved weekend visits to other corps, Freda often had to stay at home, but wherever possible we went as a family.

The boys now prefer to stay with their friends at their own corps, and throughout the years we have been blessed in each appointment in finding the right person who would open their home to them in our absence. But we try to get a balance even on this so that we are not both away too often. Our present appointment involves a good deal of long-distance travelling. Sometimes Freda and I travel together—but equally often we do our official travelling 'in turns', so that one of us can keep the family life and routine going.

Getting the balance as near right as possible is, I suppose, a matter of meeting each situation as sensibly as possible when it arises. In our present circumstances we often plan the day ahead over breakfast. Sometimes it is like a major military operation to have mum, dad, two boys, one car, two further meals and a variety of commitments coincide or dovetail, but we are frequently amazed at what can be achieved with a little bit of ingenuity.

Both Freda and I find it difficult to remember the days when we were single. Our lives seem to have been intertwined as far back as memory will go. And when we gather for the evening meal, which at present is the main family event of the day, and talk over the day's events and perhaps plan some family excursion or other, it is not only us two who give thanks to God for each other—it is a foursome.

For discussion

Freda and John, like many of our contributors, are Salvation Army officers. Do you think it is important for a wife to have a work role of her own and a certain amount of independence? (See the Subject Index under *role of the wife.*)

Discuss how this family cope with a busy schedule. (See the Subject Index under *Salvation Army family.*)

17

Hope and Stuart

Captain and Mrs Munemo (Zimbabwe)

'OUR life together began when we met for the first time, in 1972. However, ours is a life-story that requires both of us to talk about it. Hope, would you like to say a bit about yourself?'

'I am the eldest child of a family of six. My parents were divorced in 1966 when I was 14 years old. It was, however, through the influence of my mother, a methodist, that I accepted Jesus Christ as my personal Saviour. I was then brought up by a step-mother, under difficult circumstances. I became a salvationist in 1970, and God called me in 1971 to enter the officers' training college in 1973 as a member of the Followers of Christ Session. Would you like to tell about yourself, Stuart?'

'Yes. I am the eldest child of a family of eight. My parents were forbidden to marry because of tribal custom. As I was born outside wedlock, my grandfather, on my mother's side, had to bring me up. After a few years in industry I was converted in a tent mission under the ministry of the Dorothea Mission. I joined the Army where my mother had been a soldier for some time. I heard the call of God in 1967, entered training for officership the following year in the Undaunted Session and was commissioned in 1970. It was in 1972 when I was stationed in my second appointment at Ruvinga Corps, that we first met each other. Is that correct, Hope?'

'Yes. I was then living with my parents at Disi Store where father was a shopkeeper. The day we met I had gone to the district commissioner's office for a birth certificate. What were you doing, Stuart, that day?'

'I was doing my visitation rounds with Captain Solomon Matura when we met you. I really fell in love with you the first time I saw you. Something inside me told me you were the right one, although I did not say anything. But I asked for your address, name and the corps you attended. I am glad you gave me those because it was so easy for me to do a follow-up on you!'

118

'What steps did you take, Stuart, after our first meeting? It seemed you reappeared after some weeks, when I had forgotten all about you.'

'Oh, well, as an officer I sought to follow the correct Army procedure; therefore all the time I was away from you I was seeking permission from my divisional commander to court you! The moment I mentioned your name to them they remembered you and made their recommendations to me, which were favourable, and encouraged me to fall in love with you. From the divisional commander I went to talk about you with Envoy Chisango who was then in charge of your corps. He is the one who told me more about what kind of person you are and I am glad he told me the truth about you. It was not by accident that I married you, Hope, but after receiving guidance from God and my spiritual leaders. Do you still want to hear what happened later?'

'Yes, go on. I am enjoying listening to you!'

'I asked the envoy to take me to your father because I felt your father should grant me permission to approach you for courtship. According to our customs it is unusual, as you know, for a man to ask his prospective father-in-law for permission in that respect. However, I must say your father proved to me that he is a man of great understanding. It was after his consent that I came to you with my message of love. Incidentally, do you still remember that it took me about three months' visiting and writing you letters before you actually said that you loved me?'

'Yes, I do. Actually, I had been praying to God to show me his will. I needed a good life-partner for marriage, and when you approached me I needed confirmation from God.'

'Hope, when I asked you to join with me in the life partnership as officers in the Army, I noticed that you became so excited about the whole idea; could you tell me why?'

'Well, my dear, God had called me long before I met you. He wanted me to be his messenger to take the word of salvation to the people. But I was not so sure whether God wanted to send me as single or married. I needed a directive from him. I prayed about it and felt that marriage was the right thing for me in his service. That is the reason why I loved you. God directed me to you because he knew you would be the right one for me. This has not worked in vain, for I am finding fulfilment in our God-appointed marriage. I have no regrets that I married you!'

'Seeing that you were the bride would you re-tell the events of our wedding?'

'When the two years of training and spiritual enrichment came to an end my mind was focused on our forthcoming wedding. It was

1974 at Chinhoyi. The quietness in the Army hall at that time frightened me but I had to stand it. The hall was filled to capacity because many people had never attended an Army officers' wedding before. In fact, I heard some saying, "We want to see what an Army officers' wedding is like." So I became aware that many people were watching me. I felt so small in the hall; however, God gave me strength. By the way, Stuart, did you notice that when you and the best man walked into the hall the congregation remained seated and when I came in with my party everyone in the hall stood up. It was such an honour to me that I can hardly forget. However, one thought came to me: "I am going to leave my family and give up my surname! Huuuu. . . ." At first I did not like the idea, but when I realised the kind of life I was entering into I took courage to stand by my decision of marriage and walked straight to where I was directed to sit. I shall always remember the two little girls holding flowers and dressed in yellow hand-made dresses walking in short steps ahead of me, the three bridesmaids all dressed in an Army uniform matching mine, all giving me moral support. I had a beautiful white sash made specially for me; it hung from the shoulder-blade to the hem of the tunic across my chest. I held a bunch of flowers in my hands and I also had white gloves. Can you remember anything more of what took place that day, Stuart?'

'Yes, I remember the opening words of Major Svend Björndal: "It is a happy day for our two comrades who are being united today. Let us pray for the work which is before us." And a brief prayer was given. I felt relieved from my tenseness. Psalm 23 sounded completely new to me as it was read for the occasion, particularly the portion, "He leadeth me beside the still waters. He restoreth my soul. . . ." The idea of newness of life became real to me as we were starting a new way of life—you and I, as husband and wife. Which of the marriage vows sticks out most in your memory as you recall that day, Hope?'

'Do you know, Stuart, I nearly burst into tears when I said to you, "I take you for my lawful wedded husband. . . ." I had to take control of myself and tell myself that it was not a day of sorrow but of happiness. I could see my aunt with tears rolling down her cheeks. Another thing I can remember is the word of advice which was given by your aunt when she stood up and said that there should not be anything secret to the other. What is known to Hope should be known to Stuart, be it pleasant or unpleasant; share the secrets of your home and joy will come. You will learn to understand and forgive each other whenever there is trouble. I think we have tried to maintain that standard. But we must not forget the excitement in the people we found gathered at my home at Zvimba for the first reception. And even before that, do you recall that you had forgotten your tunic at Chinhoyi where we had lunch, and you had to drive back 10 miles to fetch it?'

'Oh, yes, Hope. It was so painful when I remembered it and had to return all the way to Chinhoyi. I felt much shame when I learnt that the whole schedule ran late because of me! But, all the same, it was a great thrill for me to meet so many people waiting for our arrival, singing and dancing joyfully. A question has always come to mind which I have wanted to ask you, Hope. How did your parents manage to feed the crowd of people which gathered to celebrate our wedding?'

'Sadza was cooked in a drum, a cow was killed to provide meat. Pots of cooked rice, vegetables and the lot were prepared for the people. What we ate as newly-weds was specially prepared for us and our bridal party. Father told me he had to save his two months' salary to meet the expenses!'

'That was a great honour! You know, Hope, I find it hard to forget the spirit people entered into when giving the presents they brought to us. The announcement of each gift was accompanied by shouting, whistling, dancing and singing. But the most precious gift we cherish is *The Living Bible* we received from the late Commissioner Frederick Adlam. Don't you agree?'

'I do agree. It equips us with another translation of the Bible, and it has helped us in our sermon preparation to this day. What would you say about the cake ceremony we had after the reception at Zvimba, Stuart?'

'The cake ceremony is a time of counselling and when relatives give helpful advice. The sweet cake represented the sweetness of our home and as it was passed around to everyone, so our good home was to be an example to those who would see us.'

'Hope, at our wedding we prayed for unity in our new home. And that prayer has been fulfilled. I definitely think that the unity we have in our home is the result of prayer to God and also the wise advice and counselling we received on our wedding day. I now see the importance of counselling young people before and after the wedding. As I put a piece of cake into your mouth and you put a piece into mine it was an outward expression of love to each other, but it has grown deeper and more meaningful through our daily experience as husband and wife. This has not only revolved around the two of us but has extended to our families as well. Do you notice, Hope, that I get on well with your father, mother and all your relatives, and I enjoy being in their company? And I have seen you doing the same with my parents and relatives.

'That is what it should be like, Stuart. Many problems in married life are caused by relatives, especially if they are not given a warm reception. Their age, temperament and different personalities should not influence us to dislike them. We should continue to love them the same. Your relatives and mine have all come here to visit us at different times but we have never complained to them, and now see what a reputation we have managed to build amongst them. It is fantastic! If we shake them by our behaviour to them, then in return they will shake our marriage. I have seen where this has happened and it's dreadful.'

'Talking more about our marriage, one can hardly forget the experience we had when we had travelled by night, according to the custom after the cake ceremony, to our corps. The day concluded with a message from the Lord, wasn't it so, Hope?'

'Oh, the Malunga case was carefully timed. We had planned to rest in our new home for the night after the second reception and I remember word coming for us from the local hospital at Mangula asking if the bride and bridegroom would visit a sick man at the point of death. The man was once a corps sergeant-major at the corps and had fallen from God's grace before he became ill and his name was John Malunga. His last words to us keep ringing in my ears, "I let down my Jesus!" You recall that he said these words earnestly, sincerely and repeatedly, until you said to him, "Make your confession to the Lord and the Lord is kind enough to forgive you." The tears rolled down his face as you stood by his bed praying for him. I saw his face calm down; perhaps he then understood the meaning of forgiveness and was already experiencing peace in his heart. Having seen that, shouldn't we say our marriage started with leading a seeker to the throne of God, although John Malunga died the following day?'

'Now we have been married almost 10 years, what do you see to be the value of marriage, Stuart?'

'I see marriage as God's plan. It is a triangle covenant in which man and wife have a duty towards God. Each partner covenants with God and seeks God's choice for a suitable partner who also enters into covenant with God, and the triangle is complete. Today people do not fear God and constantly the covenant solemnly made is broken without any consciousness of guilt. I am praying that our marriage be kept intact and our love burning for each other as it has been. Marriage provides a bridge for families to cross over and meet with other families. It serves as the only suitable provision of a home for children born in the world. And it serves also as a means to spread the word of God. Talking about children, it is my belief that children should be raised so that they are taught to love God.

The training of children in the home helps to build safe homes in the future here on earth and is also a good foundation for better relationships in the communities to come. Their training should involve moral and spiritual lessons, and children learn better by way of example. Children grow frustrated if a marriage is broken.'

'Stuart, you have touched on a subject that has brought much controversy and has led to breakdown in many marriages—children! Very few people realise that having a child or children in the home is an added blessing that comes from God. When we get married we do not know whether our marriage will be crowned by the bearing of children. A child is a gift from God. A gift is a free token of love from the giver and does not come through any form of demand. The giver gives as he pleases. After our wedding people expected us to have a child there and then, you will recall, and we also wanted it so, but we had to wait two years for reasons which only God knows. Pressures came from many sources suggesting what we were supposed to do to have a child. Others accused us of having ignored and defied the ancestral spirits by not participating in paying respect to them. They suggested ways to appease them. Others referred us to certain medical doctors. I had operations along with many other measures, but without any effect. We did a good thing by sitting together side by side and thinking about the terrible remarks people were making against us. They wanted us to blame God and try to force his hand before his own time. The resolution we undertook of having a whole night of prayer to God for a child was the correct step because that same month God heard and granted our request. For this reason we called our daughter Rutendo (faith). God gave us another blessing before we asked for another child and we called him Jonathan Tapfuma, for God enriched us. The words of the song which says, "He giveth more grace as our burdens grow greater . . . he giveth and giveth and giveth again" have been proved true to us. And since we have now a daughter and a son I think it has pleased God that we end there. I praise God for giving me a husband like you who understands.'

'Of course, Hope, how could I stand a situation where I would be left only with two children without a mother! When we made an attempt to have a third child you ended up nearly dead at the hospital and I thank God you and I have prayerfully agreed to be content with the two children God has given us.

'Although many African families haven't accepted people who end up with fewer children, we are glad to be among the number that have followed that way. Children need proper food, clothing, education and important lessons that concern life, and these can best be applied to a family reasonably smaller.

123

'Hope, what advice would you give to young people planning for marriage?'

'Well, Stuart, I would tell them that we do not marry to divorce but to stay as husband and wife "till death us do part". Much care should be taken before young people enter into a marriage commitment. Divorce is the destruction of all that is good under the marriage covenant. It is lack of love between the two, and this is caused by many factors: some marry for economic reasons—rich possessions to be acquired through marriage; some marry for social reasons—to be among the higher class; others prefer self-styled "marriages" which are short-lived; others marry too young; some marry under pressure without proper love; some marry because they admire the beautiful clothes on the person or facial beauty which is irrelevant. If the above is not carefully avoided then trouble follows. The family suffers and a sacred covenant is breached. There is emotional damage to the persons involved—sense of failure, lack of ability to trust other people and bitterness and insecurity within the parties. There is also material damage to be incurred—the expense of running two homes, the division of property; in some cases enmity is created between the spouses' families. Would you have any more to add to causes of divorce, Stuart?'

'Untruthfulness when making the promises; others find that they fail to get what they wanted from the person they married; sometimes it is the lack of adequate teaching about the privileges and responsibilities involved in marriage; others do not communicate well, they do not talk to each other about their problems; they do not want to speak their mind. Some problems have arisen from watching silly films on television and wrong ideas on 'love' obtained through poor books.

'Hope, do you sometimes feel I am married more to the Army than I am to you?'

'Yes, Stuart, but we are proud to belong to the Army and to be an Army couple and an Army family. As an Army couple we share many happy occasions in our service to the Lord. We give thanks to God also for being Salvation Army officers. In moments of hardship we stand side by side giving each other moral and spiritual support. We willingly accept corrections from each other, and this, I must say, is helping us to improve our standard of living daily, and is also our commitment to God's way. We are a couple who love the Lord and the Army, and many times, you will agree with me, Stuart, we have jealously guarded the Army from being injured by its foes. It has always been our desire that the gospel of Jesus Christ be interpreted in truth to all age groups and people of all

124

classes. Furthermore, what we are is what God wants, with a single desire to keep on growing in his strength as a family that loves God. We cannot say our life would have been better if we had stayed single. Could we claim that, Stuart?'

'Not by any means. In fact, we have managed to face many challenges in life, being a family, and succeeded. Although marriage is God's institution I must admit we are benefiting tremendously from it! The enjoyment I find in marriage is God's gift to me and I am grateful for it. You have counselled me on many occasions of crisis and I have done the same for you, an intimacy I would not have found anywhere the same way. We stay together and speak the same language, understanding each other, and this is a blessing indeed.'

For discussion

Hope and Stuart waited for some time before their longed-for first child was born. Discuss their feelings about this and how they reacted. (See the Subject Index under *childlessness*.)

Also, do you remember Hope describing her feelings on her wedding day? Discuss how far we give up our individual identity when we marry.

(See the Subject Index under *role of wife*.)

125

18

Lise and Siegfried
Major and Mrs Clausen (Spain)

LONDON Transport was on strike when the cadets of the Courageous Session left the ITC, and we all departed as best we could, some by train, others on foot or by any other means.

I was standing on the steps seeing everybody off, when suddenly our training principal called me aside and told me to leave through the back entrance and go out through the back gate and down a small alley. Somebody would be waiting for me there. I was not due to leave till next day, but even so I obeyed when I saw the twinkle in Commissioner Westergaard's eye, and I went to find that he had directed a young man lieutenant to the same spot—and so Siegfried and I were able to walk together to the station to say goodbye. Twenty-five years have gone since that day, and we have walked a long way since then, through foreign lands, beautiful forests, by the seaside of the Pacific Ocean, the Atlantic, the Mediterranean, through deserts, on the Altiplano, the Andes Mountains, even flat Denmark as well as Germany and England—and now lately in Spain, but always together because that gives us strength.

Straight after training our ways parted for some short years. Siegfried was sent to Germany after a short period in England, and I went back to my home country, Denmark, already sure that God wanted me to go to South America. That is where we met again, when Siegfried arrived back to the country where he was born, and where I had already been made very much at home during the nine months I had been serving there.

Our courtship was not the happiest period in our lives. We were too busy. Being officers meant a lot of responsibilities and our real understanding of each other did not commence till we married on 31 March 1962.

For a couple of months Siegfried had been the corps officer at Santiago Central Corps, Chile, with two girl lieutenants as his assistants. I was one of the girls, and so on our wedding day, as

126

friends decorated our hall, I spent the morning cleaning and ironing our uniforms while Siegfried moved his belongings to the quarters where we girls were already living. The rest of the day we were surrounded by friends and relatives (Siegfried's family) and it was a happy day with lots of fun, the warmth of Salvation Army fellowship, a solemn ceremony, and we were indeed happy.

The years that followed brought us much joy in our family life. God gave us two children, Carl and Ingrid, and certainly much fulfilment in our life as a Salvation Army family. Different appointments taught us to adjust to different circumstances, often sharing our own private life with others. When serving on the training college in Chile, while the children were still small, I remember having to pass the penitent form at night in the darkness, whenever the children called from their bedroom opposite ours with the hall in between. I soon learned to avoid the penitent form in the darkness, after a few bruises! But then I also learnt to use it as my place for private devotions.

While we were in Bolivia, the women cadets lived in our sitting room, and often, very often, we have felt the need to be alone as a family. Probably that is always why we enjoy being together, and it is a special treat to come home after a journey or even after a long day's work. Our home has become our refuge. As our children grow they become very much involved in Salvation Army activities, and we thoroughly enjoy being an Army family, always trying to emphasise the purpose of our activities, and not being involved because of the activity alone.

We are convinced there is nothing that can replace the influence of Christian family life. It is not enough just to be 'Army'—the Christlike way of living has to be practised at home, and it is a plus for all the members of a family to share and enjoy this experience. Because of it we are all better fitted to face the daily routine of life and know our priorities.

After 17 years in South America, where we felt completely at home, and where Siegfried and the children were born, we faced a change to Europe. We soon found out that the country where we lived did not accept our marriage as legal, and so one day Siegfried came home and asked me if I would marry him again! By then, our children were 16 and 12 years old, and they quickly started to take advantage of the situation, talking about their 'first' mother who was young and slim and patient and so on! There was not a moment of doubt as far as my answer was concerned. This time both of us knew what we were in for and realised that the years had changed our relationship to a very deep love and understanding, a complete sharing in confidence.

The years in Europe proved to be completely different from our former life of service and activities, and we are quite sure that the reason why we have been able to face this change, which we neither wanted nor accepted willingly, has been because of the strength we have found in being together.

Highlights of our married life have often been very ordinary moments, occasions where we have needed each other's comprehension and where we have been able to find in each other the deep fellowship and love which meant the answer to our need—a few moments just for ourselves have done wonders.

To be married has certainly enriched our personal lives—and enabled us to grow spiritually—often finding encouragement and strength in our union, feeling that our love for each other has also meant a greater understanding of God's love towards us. God brought us together from lands apart, and his timing was perfect. He has led us through our marriage and our years as a family, and we trust him for the future.

We might even have the occasion of marrying again for the third time in a different country—we shall be happy to do so!

For discussion

Lise and Siegfried emphasise the need for a married couple (or a family) to have moments of privacy. Discuss the concept of the home as a 'refuge'.

(See the Subject Index under *home*.)

Appendices

The Salvation Army Articles of Marriage

(a) We do solemnly declare that we have not sought this marriage for the sake of our own happiness and interests only, although we believe these will be furthered thereby.

(b) We promise that we will not allow our marriage in any way to lessen our devotion to God and our service in The Salvation Army.

(c) We promise that we will use all our influence with each other to promote our constant and entire self-sacrifice for the salvation of the world.

(d) We promise to make our quarters (home) a place where all shall be aware of the abiding presence of God and to train those under our influence for faithful service to him in the Army.

(e) We promise never to allow the cause of God to be injured or hindered in any of its interests without doing our utmost to prevent it.

(f) We promise should either of us from sickness, death or any other cause cease to be an efficient soldier that the remaining one shall continue to the best of his or her ability to fulfil all these undertakings.

Marriage and divorce statistics, 1979

THE following tables have been compiled from official government statistics of the countries listed. The most recent figures for international comparison at the time of writing are for 1979. Table 1 gives an indication of the numbers involved, whilst Table 2 adopts the 'per 1000 of population' form which is the normal method of making comparisons between countries in this field. It should be noted that the tables offer only a broad picture. To determine the number of marriages ending in divorce, records would have to be kept over a very long period of time. The right-hand column in each table shows the divorces taking place in 1979. Hardly any of these would have involved those married in that year, shown in the left-hand column.

Table 1—total numbers

Country	Marriages	Divorces
Australia	104,396	37,854
Austria	45,188	12,956
Belgium	65,476	13,499
Denmark	27,842	13,044
England and Wales	368,854	138,706
Finland	29,277	10,191
France	340,405	79,800
Jamaica	8,949	756
Japan	788,505	135,250
Netherlands	85,648	23,748
Norway	23,055	6,608
Sweden	37,300	20,322
Switzerland	33,987	10,394
USA	2,331,337	1,181,000

Table 2—per 1000 population

Country	Marriages	Divorces
Australia	7.2	2.6
Austria	6.0	1.72
Belgium	6.6	1.37
Denmark	5.4	2.55
England and Wales	7.5	2.8
Finland	6.1	2.14
France	6.4	1.69
Jamaica	4.2	0.35
Japan	6.8	1.17
Netherlands	6.1	2.86
Norway	5.7	1.62
Sweden	4.5	2.45
Switzerland	5.3	1.63
USA	10.6	5.3

Not every country issues statistics. For instance, no figures are available for the Congo, and in Malaysia the figures are available at the discretion of the government only in response to a written request with reasons for wanting them. Some countries have no provision in their laws for divorce and so no statistics are produced, eg Italy, Portugal, Spain, Chile and The Philippines. These are predominantly Roman Catholic countries. In South Africa the published figures relate only to white, coloured and Asian members of the population. No statistics for black South Africans are available.

Table 2 gives a rough indication that marriage generally is more stable in, for instance, Jamaica and Japan, and less stable in, for instance, Sweden and the USA. The American divorce statistics include also annulments (when the law decrees there never has been a valid marriage, as opposed to a divorce when the law decrees that a valid marriage is now terminated).

Much interesting, but perhaps alarming, data is published by the USA in *National Estimates of Marriage—Dissolution and Survivorship*, published by the US Department of Health and Human Services (1980). In the States it is estimated that on the wedding day a marriage has a 47.4 per cent chance of ending in divorce. The chances decline as the marriage matures so that after 10 years the chance is 25.9 per cent and after 20 years is 10.9 per cent and so on.

In England and Wales the divorce rate for those marrying aged less than 20 years is double the rate for those who marry aged 20 or older.

The Salvation Army

Positional Statement on Marriage (1983)

THE Salvation Army affirms the New Testament standard of marriage, that is, the voluntary and loving union for life of one man and one woman to the exclusion of all others, this union being established by an authorised ceremony.

'Voluntary' indicates that the parties freely choose or, in some cultures, agree to enter into the marriage. 'For life' indicates there can be no such thing as a trial or temporary marriage. 'One man and one woman' means that marriage is possible only between members of the opposite sex, and 'to the exclusion of all others' stresses the fidelity inherent in the marriage bond.

By its nature, marriage rests on a relationship of love, a reflection of God's love for the human race. The permanence of the marriage bond provides for security and developing mutual trust, referred to in Scripture as a 'one flesh' relationship (Genesis 2:24, Ephesians 5:21-23), which Jesus affirmed: 'What therefore God hath joined together, let not man put asunder' (Matthew 19:6).

The exclusive nature of marriage leaves no room for sexual infidelity. In sexual intercourse spouses express to one another profound feelings of love, mutual respect, inter-dependence and belonging. Sexual relations outside marriage will always fall short of this. Only assurance of each other's total loyalty leads to the proper growth of the marriage relationship.

The Salvation Army asserts that God's standard concerning marriage, revealed in Scripture, pertains to all people everywhere. Jesus taught that divorce is failure (Mark 10:2-12; Matthew 19:3-12). Salvationists believe, however, that his attitude to those caught up in marital strife would never be anything but loving and compassionate.

Therefore, The Salvation Army, whilst defending vigorously the ongoing relevance of God's will for men and women in relation to marriage, recognises the reality that some marriages fail and is willing, under God, to offer counsel and succour to couples so affected. Where remarriage could lead to the healing of emotional wounds, the Army will permit its officers to perform a marriage ceremony for a divorced person. Sound doctrine with practical mercy are the hall-marks of the salvationist's approach to marital and emotional strife.

The Salvation Army reasserts that the strengthening and encouragement of the institution of marriage remains an essential pre-condition for sound family life which is, in turn, crucial to a stable society.

Extract from *Orders and Regulations for Corps Officers of The Salvation Army* (1976)

THE following extract sets out briefly a corps officer's responsibilities with regard to the marriages of those in his care or under his command. It is a regulation to which normally only officers would have access, but lay salvationists will benefit from knowing clearly the sort of demands placed upon a corps officer and may feel less inhibited about discussing with him or her realistically and in confidence matters connected with courtship, marriage and family life.

Preparation for marriage

1 A corps officer will accept responsibility for those salvationists who are courting or engaged, by seeking to help prepare them for marriage. The Christian standard for marriage is a life-long partnership. They should be taught to anticipate the emotional adjustments that will need to be made.

Officer's responsibility

2 Couples should be encouraged to face the issues that are likely to arise in the marriage relationship. These will include career and financial problems; health and biological matters; questions about children and the responsibilities of parenthood; what to do about misunderstandings; similarities and differences in habits, interests and religious faith; secret fears, guilt, and the recurring need of forgiveness; uncertainties about relatives and in-laws; the Christian home and spiritual devotion; Salvation Army commitments.

Issues to face

3 There may be separate conversations with the prospective husband and wife, but a number of joint meetings is desirable. The couple need to learn, at the outset of their life together, to show consideration for each other and to reveal the outgoing nature of love.

Before marriage

4 A visit early in a couple's married life is imperative. Many of the difficulties and tendencies that prevent marital success appear in the first few weeks. The early facing of these may be decisive for the future.

After marriage

5 When counselling, an officer should remember that:

Essential points

(a) A good marriage has to be worked at. It is an achievement, not a gift.

(b) Marriage is a partnership which should relate to every aspect of life.

(c) Married love should be 'balanced love'. When children arrive there should be no withdrawal of the wife's love for her husband. On the other hand, as work responsibilities increase,

134

there should not be a total absorption in business affairs by the husband.
(d) While frank discussion is necessary in any developing relationship, an attitude of intolerance needs to be guarded against.
(e) Questions relating to the parents of the couple should be thoroughly discussed.
(f) To integrate sex and love is fundamental.

Marriage

1 The stability of his people's marriages is part of a corps officer's responsibility. Tensions arise in all marriages, including those of Christians, and salvationists should therefore be encouraged to seek any needed help.

Tensions

2 It is generally understood that there are two periods when marriages are particularly threatened: namely, the first few years, and later, when the couple are middle-aged and children are grown up. An understanding of these critical phases could help in the task of preventing marital breakdown.

Periods particularly threatened

3 The chief causes of breakdown are:

Causes of breakdown

(a) Failure in communication. Married people need to talk about every aspect of their relationship. But in addition to verbal communication there needs to be emotional communication, that is, relating to each other at the level of feeling. If this dual kind of communication is maintained, the sexual relationship usually develops satisfactorily.

(b) Personality problems. Sometimes people of very different personality traits marry. Such marriages can be satisfactory provided both partners can make the necessary adjustments. If, however, the ability to adjust is limited, there are bound to be underlying tensions.

(c) Varied approaches to marriage. A couple may bring different expectations into the relationship. Everyone is the product of an individual home situation, and tends to expect marriage to conform to the pattern that is familiar.

(d) External pressures. These may include inadequate housing, financial worries, problems with relations, difficulties caused by work.

(e) Quarrels. Differences of opinion are bound to emerge, but these need not lead to quarrelling. Some people can tolerate much more tension than others. The causes of disagreements need to be identified and clarified. The right kind of communication needs to be encouraged.

(f) Sexual difficulties. In many instances an open sharing of problems can point the way to their solution. Sometimes, however, expert help is needed.

4 An officer will be aware of the dangers involved in counselling one partner without the other; both must be included.

Both partners

5 The Christian standard of chastity before marriage and fidelity within marriage is basic to Army thinking and teaching.

Chastity and fidelity

135

Useful Reading

THE following books are recommended as good, easy reading and are written by Christians:

Marriage Without Pretending
  Anne Townsend (Scripture Union)

Starting Out Together
  Gavin Reid (Hodder and Stoughton)

I Married You
  Walter Trobisch (IVP)

Getting Married in Church
  Mary Batchelor (Lion Publishing)

Passages
  Gail Sheehy (E. P. Dutton Company, New York)

Mid-life: a Time to Discover, a Time to Decide
  Richard P. Olson (Judson Press, Valley Forge)

30 Critical Problems Facing Today's Family (Audio-Script)
  James Dobson (Word, Inc, Waco, Texas)

Communication—Key to Your Marriage:
  H. Norman Wright (Regal Books, Glendale, California)

Handbook for Engaged Couples, A
  Robert and Alice Fryling (IVP, Downers Grove, Illinois, USA)

How to Have a Happy Marriage
  David and Vera Mace (Abingdon Press, USA)

L'amour est un sentiment qui doit s'apprendre
  Walter Trobisch (IVP)

Premarital Counselling—a Guide Book for the Counsellor
  H. Norman Wright (Moody Press, USA)

Sexual Understanding Before Marriage
  Herbert J. Miles (Zondervan Books, USA)

Strike the Original Match
  Charles R. Swindall (World Wide Publications, Minneapolis, USA)

Two Into One
  Joyce Huggett (IVP)

What's Happening to Clergy Marriages?
  David and Vera Mace (Abingdon, USA)

(The last two books concentrate on the marriages of ministers of religion)

Contributors

Shaw and Helen Clifton are Salvation Army officers serving at International Headquarters in London where Captain Clifton is the Legal Secretary. They are graduates of the University of London and have served as officers in the United Kingdom and in Zimbabwe. They have two children, Matthew and Jenny, and have been married for 17 years. They have jointly edited the material for *Growing Together*.

Ed Dawkins was commissioned an officer of the Army in 1953 and married his wife, Desley, in 1959. They have three children and have recently become grandparents. Major Dawkins is State Social Services Secretary, New South Wales, Australia. He and his wife are experienced marriage enrichment group leaders and have served in a variety of appointments in The Salvation Army's social services in the Australia Eastern Territory.

Philip and Keitha Needham have two children, Heather Lea and Holly Dawn, and are serving at The Salvation Army's divisional headquarters in North Carolina, USA. They have been married for 21 years. Major Needham is a graduate of Princeton Theological Seminary and both he and his wife hold degrees from the University of Miami in Florida. Each has long experience in pastoral caring and marriage counselling.

David and Alice Baxendale serve as Salvation Army officers at territorial headquarters in California, USA Western Territory. They have long experience of serving the Lord in the Army and have become well-known amongst American salvationists for their family-life seminars. They have been married for 30 years and have three children. Colonel Baxendale studied at Springfield College, Massachusetts and at the Teachers' College, Columbia. Mrs Baxendale studied at Syracuse University, New York.

Sidney Gauntlett, who was awarded the MBE in 1959, is Medical Adviser to the Salvation Army Social Services in Great Britain and Ireland as well as Director of Alcoholism and Counselling Services. He studied medicine in London and served in India, Zambia and Nigeria at Salvation Army medical centres with his first wife, Violet, who died in 1975. For many years Lieut-Colonel Gauntlett has been involved in marital counselling and sex education. He was formerly psychiatric adviser and counsellor to two Salvation Army schools for young offenders and has worked with a drug-dependants' programme in the West End of London where the results of marital breakdown were starkly apparent. He has two children. He married Jean, his present wife, six years ago, following the tragic death of his second wife, Edith, from cancer after less than a year of marriage.

Dr and Mrs (Dr) Kildahl-Andersen are salvationists in Norway and are members of the Army corps at Trondheim. They have two young sons, Arne and Geir, and have been married for 10 years. Mrs Kildahl-Andersen is a qualified nurse and is senior registrar in a department of the Trondheim Regional Hospital. Dr Kildahl-Andersen studied medicine in the University of Iceland and in 1983 became a research fellow of the Norwegian Cancer Society. He is a member of the permanent staff of the Trondheim Regional Hospital.

Pat Hill has served, with her husband, Harold, as a Salvation Army officer and doctor in both Zimbabwe and New Zealand. Captain and Mrs Hill have been married for 12 years and have two daughters, Ruth and Mary. Prior to her marriage Mrs Hill served at the Chikankata Hospital in Zambia, having studied medicine in

Dunedin and London. At present they are the corps officers at Invercargill, New Zealand. Mrs Hill is also a part-time medical officer with the New Zealand Department of Health, dealing mainly with children and family situations.

Margaret Mead and her husband, Colin, have three children: teenagers Tracy and Darryl, and Hayley who is nine years old. The whole family belong to the Johannesburg City Corps where Mrs Mead teaches the Bible class for teenagers. She is involved in the 'Renewing Love' tape ministry to women and lectures at The Salvation Army's officer training college and elsewhere on marriage and personal relationships. Margaret and Colin have been married for almost 20 years.

Lee Fisher is a psychologist, preacher, lecturer, writer and counsellor. He is the director of the guidance and counselling centre at Asbury College in Wilmore, Kentucky. He also teaches part-time in the psychology department. Professor Fisher travels extensively in the USA and Canada leading youth retreats, summer camp seminars, marriage and family seminars, officers' councils and many other gatherings organised by The Salvation Army. He is a member of the Christian Association for Psychological Studies and, as an active salvationist, contributes a regular advice column to *The War Cry* in the USA.

Ted and Dianne Palmer married 22 years ago and have three children: Grant, Tanya and Christopher. Both are university graduates and have served as Salvation Army officers in Canada for many years, mostly in evangelical and pastoral positions. They lead marriage encounter seminars and are the authors of *Full-Time Families,* a guide to Christian family life, published by The Salvation Army in Canada.

Joseph and Mary Larbi are Salvation Army officers in Ghana. They have four children: Emmanuel, John, Felicia and Margaret, and have been married for 21 years. Captain Larbi is the divisional commander in the East Akim Division. The Larbis have wide experience of meeting and counselling married couples and families in crisis.

Freddy and Anna Münch are in charge of The Salvation Army's officer training college in the Congo. They have also served in France, the land of their birth. For seven years they were closely involved with young people, being responsible for an Army youth centre. Major Münch worked for the French Ministry of Agriculture in Cameroun before becoming a Salvation Army officer. Mrs Münch is a certificated youth worker. They have been married for 27 years and have three children.

Jinichi and Shigeko Osato live and work in Kiryu, Japan. They have a son, Tadahiro, and a daughter, Kyoko. They married 23 years ago. Mr Osato holds a Master of Education degree and is a former school principal. He is now the teachers' consultant at the Education Research Institute in Kiryu, specialising in pupil-problems and relationships in both the school and the home. He is the young people's·sergeant-major in the Kiryu Corps and Mrs Osato helps with the home league. Tadahiro and Kyoko are also involved in the corps, teaching in the Sunday-school and participating in musical activity.

Emmanuel and Rashidan Iqbal have long and varied experience as Salvation Army officers in Pakistan. Major Iqbal has a Bachelor of Arts degree and both he and his wife have undergone training courses in London. They have four children, two girls and two boys. Following an appointment as the divisional commander in Lahore, the major is now principal of the officer training college in Pakistan.

John and Freda Larsson have served as Salvation Army officers both in England and Scotland. They have recently left Chile where Lieut-Colonel Larsson was Chief Secretary for the South America West Territory. He is a graduate of the University of London. Lieut-Colonel and Mrs Larsson have been married for 15 years and have two sons, Karl and Kevin.

Stuart and Hope Munemo are Salvation Army officers in Zimbabwe where Captain Munemo is presently studying at the University of Zimbabwe. They have been officers for 14 years, serving in corps appointments before moving to the officer training college and later to territorial headquarters where Captain Munemo had oversight of the Army's youth work throughout Zimbabwe. They have two young children, Rutendo and Jonathan.

Siegfried and Lise Clausen are in charge of Salvation Army work in Spain. Major Clausen was born in Chile of German parents whilst Mrs Clausen comes from Denmark. Together, in 22 years of married life, they have served in Chile, Bolivia, Germany, the United Kingdom and Spain. They have a daughter, Ingrid, still at school and a son, Carl, who works in London and is a member of the Army corps at Chalk Farm.

Index of Bible References

142

Subject Index

This index is intended to be helpful not only for the general reader but also for *groups wishing to discuss a particular topic.* Some of the subjects are dealt with only in passing, but even this may be enough to spark off discussion within the group.

A

Abortion, 7
Adapting to one another, 5, 14, 57–58, 65–66, 107, 134–135
Adoption and fostering, 48
Adultery (see also *Fidelity*), 42–44, 68
Alcohol, 19, 77, 89
Anger, 62–63, 85, 86
Apologising, 37, 55–56
Arranged marriage, 113, 114 (see also note under *Relatives*)

B

Bereavement, 75–78
Boredom, 26, 67
Booth, William, 95
Boy–girl relationships, 3–5

C

Childbirth, 40–41, 52–53
Childlessness, 47–48, 123
Children, 15, 84–87, 91, 123

Note: This book has not dealt with the specialised subject of the problems of having in the family a child with a physical or mental handicap. Discussion groups may well want to explore the topic, especially where one of the group is parent to such a child and can therefore grant valuable insights to the others. (*Eds.*)

Cohabitation, 7, 9
Commitment, 5, 20, 62
Communication, 54–60, 85, 120, 128, 135

R

Redundancy, 78–80
Relatives, 15–16, 64–65, 113–114, 119, 121–122, 135

Note: More could be said about the problems of arranged marriages in families where young adults want more freedom. Much sorrow is caused when parents are too harsh in this matter. Recently in England, three Indian girls committed suicide together in a car, following a family dispute about arranged marriages (*The Times,* 3 May 1984). In the same newspaper, there was a feature on family attitudes in Northern Ireland to Protestant/Roman Catholic marriages. 'Tread softly' is a good maxim here. (*Eds.*)

Re-marriage after divorce, 133
Role of the wife, 11–12, 37, 69–70, 87, 102, 116
Role of the husband, 11–12, 37, 67–68, 87, 102, 116

S

Salvation Army corps life, 94–100
Salvation Army family life, 88–93, 94–100, 106, 111, 116–117, 124, 127
Salvation Army officership, 89–92, 97, 115-117, 134-135
Salvation Army uniform, 17, 111
Selfishness, 31, 55, 57
Sexual relationship, 6–8, 27–39, 40–46, 106, 135
Single life, 21, 115
Sunday, 98, 111

T

Trial marriage, 7, 9

U

Unemployment, 78–80

V

Venereal disease, 7
Violence, 66 (see also *Anger*)

Note: Violence in the home is a very real threat to some families. While beyond the scope of this book, the problem should nevertheless be a cause of concern to Christians. Any who find themselves either prone to violence or victims of violence should not be ashamed to seek expert help. (*Eds.*)

W

Work, 54, 58–59, 78–80